D1558997

Buckminster Fuller

PIONEERS in CHANGE

Buckminster Fuller

ROBERT R. POTTER

Silver Burdett Press
Englewood Cliffs, New Jersey

CONSULTANTS :

Loy Fook Lee, Master of Architecture Degree, Columbia University. Richard M. Haynes, Assistant Professor, Division of Administration, Curriculum, and Instruction; Director of the Office of Field Experience and Teacher Placement, School of Education and Psychology, Western Carolina University.

TEXT AND DIAGRAM CREDITS:

Pp. 8–9 (poems): Courtesy of the Buckminster Fuller Institute, Los Angeles; p. 43 (poem); From *Buckminster Fuller: At Home in the Universe*, by Alden Hatch. Copyright © 1974 by Alden Hatch. Reprinted by permission of Crown Publishers, Inc.; p. 115 (diagram based on illustration by Hugh Kenner in *Bucky: A Guided Tour of Buckminster Fuller*, by Hugh Kenner, © 1973, Morrow): Permission granted by Hugh Kenner; p. 138 (quotations in 1st paragraph): Permission granted by *The Futurist*; p. 141: Reprinted by permission; © 1983, The New Yorker Magazine, Inc.

PHOTOGRAPH ACKNOWLEDGMENTS:

Buckminster Fuller Institute, Los Angeles, © 1980: p. 78; Buckminster Fuller Institute, Los Angeles, © 1960, The Estate of Buckminster Fuller: pp. 10, 25, 31, 42, 74; James Mason/Black Star: frontispiece; St. Louis Post-Dispatch: pp. 122–123; Southern Illinois University at Carbondale: pp. 131, 139; Union Tank Car Co.: pp. 118–119; UPI/Bettmann Newsphotos: pp. 82–83, 90–91, 105, 126–127.

SERIES AND COVER DESIGN:

R STUDIO T·Raúl Rodríguez and Rebecca Tachna

ART DIRECTOR:

Linda Huber

MANAGING EDITOR :

Nancy Furstinger

PROJECT EDITOR:

Richard G. Gallin

PHOTO RESEARCH:

Omni-Photo Communications, Inc.

Copyright © 1990 by Gallin House Press, Inc.
All rights reserved including the right of reproduction
in whole or in part in any form.
Published by Silver Burdett Press, Inc., a division of
Simon & Schuster, Inc., Englewood Cliffs, NJ 07632
Manufactured in the United States of America.
ISBN 0-382-09967-2 (Lib. ed.)
10 9 8 7 6 5 4 3 2 1
ISBN 0-382-09972-9 (pbk.)
10 9 8 7 6 5 4 3 2 1

Library of Congress Cataloging-in-Publication Data

Potter, Robert R.
Buckminster Fuller / Robert R. Potter
p. cm.—(Pioneers in change)
Includes bibliographical references.
Summary: A biography of an outstanding creative thinker and designer whose inventive technological expressions were attempts to make life easier and more comfortable for people while still maintaining a close relationship with nature.
1. Fuller, R. Buckminster (Richard Buckminster), 1895–   —Juvenile literature.
2. Architecture—United States—Biography—Juvenile literature.   3. Inventors— United States—Biography—Juvenile literature.   [1. Fuller, R. Buckminster (Richard Buckminster), 1895–   .   2. Inventors.   3. Architects.]
I. Title.   II. Series.
TA140.F9P68   1990
620'.0092—dc20
[B]
[92]   90-34187
                                                                        CIP
                                                                        AC

CONTENTS

"Comfortably Off"

"I was born cross-eyed," Buckminster Fuller once wrote. "Not until I was four years old was it discovered that this was caused by my being abnormally farsighted. My vision was thereafter fully corrected with lenses. Until four I could see only large patterns, houses, trees, outlines of people with blurred coloring. While I saw two dark areas on human faces, I did not see a human eye or a teardrop or a human hair until I was four."

A plea for sympathy? No, not at all. Just the opposite. Fuller went on to explain how lucky he'd been to be born with poor sight. A fuzzy detail in his surroundings went unnoticed. This forced him to concentrate on the larger pattern, the BIG PICTURE. In later years, that became his formula for clear thinking. First you focused on the BIG PICTURE. Then you filled in the details. Thus a childhood misfortune had been turned into a blessing. *A minus had become a plus.*

Bucky Fuller was to do that many, many times in the 87 years he spent on what he called Spaceship Earth.

The BIG PICTURE of R. Buckminster Fuller? ... It's hard to explain in a paragraph. At the time of his death in 1983, he had the longest entry in *Who's Who in America*. He'd been on the cover of *Time* magazine. He'd dined with presidents. The famous geodesic dome was only one of his twenty-five patented inventions. He'd spoken at over five hundred colleges and universities, forty-seven of which had given him honorary degrees. He'd preached his upbeat message of human friendship and betterment to a whole generation of students. And for those who couldn't hear him in person, he'd written seventeen important books. In fifty-seven trips around the world, he'd become known as "the planet's friendly genius."

Architect, inventor, scientist, mathematician. Historian, economist, philosopher, prophet. Bucky Fuller was all these things—and more. Throughout his life, he shied away from the one-word labels others wanted to pin on him—just as he shrugged off labels like *crackpot* and *inspired child*. He liked to call himself a *comprehensivist*. (Fuller was forever creating new word combinations. *Comprehensive*, of course, means "including a great deal." Here he adds *ist* to make the word refer to a person, like *feminist*.)

Yet the person who perhaps best knew Fuller's mind suggests that the word to describe him is *poet*. This may be true, from the beginning (in Fuller's words):

Womb days—
Womb days—
Dear old tummy tomb days—

to the BIG PICTURE:

Environment to each must be
All Universe excepting me.
The Universe in turn must be
All that isn't me plus me.

Richard Buckminster Fuller, Jr., was born on July 12, 1895. The place: Milton, Massachusetts, a new and growing suburb of Boston. The weather: warm and sunny, with prospects clear. The family tree was a sturdy old oak. The first Fuller had come to New England in the 1630s, shortly after the Pilgrims. Years later, the Reverend Timothy Fuller represented Massachusetts at the Constitutional Convention. Timothy Fuller refused to sign the final Constitution because it permitted slavery. His grandson, the Reverend Arthur Buckminster Fuller, served as a Union chaplain during the Civil War. As a chaplain, Arthur wasn't supposed to engage in fighting himself. But his hatred of slavery was such that he insisted on leading the troops into the line of fire. A Confederate bullet ended his life at the Battle of Fredericksburg.

The most famous of Bucky's ancestors was his great-aunt, the amazing Margaret Fuller. She was a feminist before the word was known. Margaret Fuller mastered five languages before she was out of her teens. Later, with Ralph Waldo Emerson, she founded *The Dial*, a pioneering literary magazine. Then in 1845 she wrote *Woman in the Nineteenth Century*. All during her life, she held her own with the best minds of her time. (More than that, maybe. She once told Emerson, "I now know all the people worth knowing in America, and I find no intellect comparable to mine.") A great aunt indeed!

It was a family tradition for Fuller men to attend

9

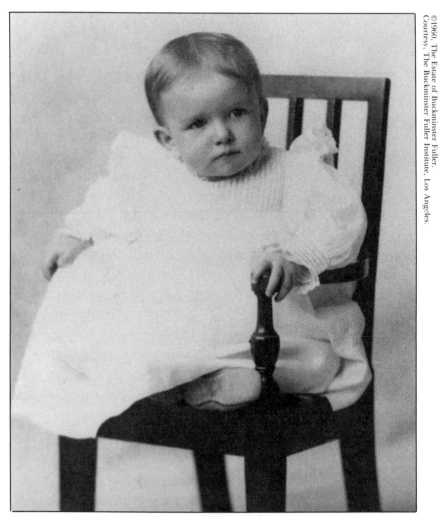

Bucky Fuller at age one.

Harvard and then become ministers or lawyers. Bucky's father, however, had followed only half of this tradition. He graduated from Harvard. He then turned his attention to the business world. In a great port city like Boston, importing goods from foreign countries had brought success to many. Richard Fuller determined to go into the import business. He made contacts. He did well. At the time of Bucky's birth, Richard Fuller's busy docks in Boston welcomed fine leathers from India and Argentina, fragrant teas from China and Ceylon.

In 1891, Richard Fuller had married Caroline Wolcott Andrews, the daughter of a well-to-do Chicago family. She, too, had a distinguished heritage. Distant ancestors had signed the Declaration of Independence and been governors of Connecticut. A year after they married, a girl, Leslie, was born. Three years later, with Bucky on the way, the successful young couple decided to go after that typical American dream, a lot and house in the suburbs. The lot in Milton turned out to be two and a half acres of wooded land, set on a bluff. The new house was a small version of a Victorian mansion: huge white fireplaces, a paneled dining room, servants' quarters in a third-floor attic. A cook was hired. A gardener tended the grounds. At times Bucky and his sister Leslie each had a private nurse.

Of course Bucky really didn't get a good look at the house until he was four and a half. Then came the glasses. Bucky was overjoyed. Now he could see the separate shingles on the house, not just a blurry wall. He could see his toenails. He could see the tiny brown hairs on his arm! He could see the cat's eyes—and outside, even the eyes of a snake! What pleased him most, though, were the eyes of his mother. There was tenderness there, concern and warmth and love.

Why, eyes could communicate! They could almost speak! It mattered little to Bucky that the thick lenses that framed his own eyes made them look larger than normal to others.

Before the glasses, Bucky was thought of as an awkward child, perhaps a little slow. Now he proved to be just the opposite: curious, bright, ever into mischief. He learned about his new surroundings with surprising speed. He learned also to stand up to Leslie, who now often viewed her brother as a new and unwanted challenge. She was forever trying to put him down.

Many of Bucky's first memories concerned his father, a gentle man to whom he was devoted. (Fuller Senior was called both Richard and Dick, and the name Buckminster just seemed too lengthy and lofty for a little kid. The boy was "Bucky" almost at birth.) "I clearly remember New Year's Eve, December 31, 1899," Bucky wrote later. "I was four and a half. I had just received my eyeglasses and was deeply excited at all that I could now see. At 11:45 P.M. my father opened a window of our New England home to let in the twentieth century." Bucky also remembered his father leading him to church by the hand, talking seriously about God, trying to interest the boy in becoming a minister. One of Bucky's main regrets was that Richard Fuller's business so often took him away from home. A trip to Argentina could take months. A trip to India once took almost a year.

Another memory—often mentioned by Bucky with some pride—concerned a happening in kindergarten. The teacher had given each child a bunch of half-dried peas and a pile of toothpicks. The kids were told to use their imaginations, to build something. Most of the children, as might be expected, made houses and barns. But not Bucky. Avoiding cubes and rectangles, he made a triangle, then seemed pleased with its rigid form. To this he attached another triangle, on the side. Then he added another triangle, and another. Before long he had a strong, complex, three-dimensional structure made entirely of triangles. The teacher was so pleased that she called other teachers into the room to look at it. This surprised Bucky, but it pleased him as well. And why did it so please Bucky to tell this story in later years? Surely, neither the teachers nor Bucky had known that his toothpicks and peas formed something very like the *octet truss* he would patent in 1961.

But the sharpest, the most meaningful, of Bucky's early memories concerned Bear Island. Throughout his life, this bit of beauty off the coast of Maine remained Bucky's hold on reality in a changing world. It gave him a sense of place— and, to him, was a place of sense.

At the turn of the century, one mark of success in life was to buy a lot in the suburbs and build a big house. Another was to take—or send—the family away for a long summer vacation. The practice was called summering. ("We live in Boston but we summer in Maine.") It still makes sense to some people today. But back in the days before air-conditioning, before even electric fans, when horses and outhouses fouled the hot air of July and August, it probably made much more sense. Better the bright mountain breezes or the fresh breath of the sea!

At first the Fullers, with other relatives, summered at Marblehead, on the Massachusetts coast north of Boston. Then it was Wiscasset, in southern Maine. Finally, in 1904, it was farther along the Maine coast, the Penobscot Bay area. Bucky's Grandmother Andrews came east from Chicago with some other relatives, and the whole clan summered on Eagle Island. They lived in a boardinghouse. For Bucky it was a summer of endless surprise, just made for a nine-year-old boy. The island was like a mountaintop rising from the surface of the water. Bucky loved climbing the black rocks, polished smooth by the waves of thousands of years. On clear days the white seagulls traced patterns against the bright blue sky. At other times the gulls fed on crabs and other delicacies of the low tide, their squabbling cries spreading over the gray-green sea.

Penobscot Bay is dotted with islands. Bucky, short for his age but wiry and strong, kept up with his older cousins in exploring them all. American Indians had once lived on the islands, and arrowheads were not hard to find. Bucky thought the local lobstermen and fishermen fascinating. They spoke in a strange way, but their gnarled hands and knowing eyes taught lessons beyond the scope of speech. Bucky loved watching them at work. He liked listening to their stories. His days were active, his sleepy nights cool. The sound of the sea, from the lapping of little waves to storm-blown billowing, was never far away.

Living close to nature taught Bucky an important lesson that was to serve him well throughout life. The fishermen sailed only when the winds were right. To predict the weather, they studied the skies. They took advantage of the unusually high tide in Penobscot Bay. Their boats were so graceful—not for the sake of art, but simply to slide through the sea. A mast bent a little in the wind; it did not stand rigid and then snap off. Bucky learned that getting along with nature did not mean fighting nature. No, it meant studying nature's ways and then cooperating with them. Human beings were part of nature, after all. They had to fit in.

Bucky was not the only one excited by that summer on Eagle Island. In fact, the whole family fell in love with the area, almost at once. Before much time had passed, Bucky's father asked Grandmother Andrews to think about buying one of several nearby islands that were for sale. She agreed. This was even more fun for Bucky—inspecting islands, one of which would be the family's very own! At length Grandmother Andrews decided on Bear Island, two miles from Eagle. Bucky could hardly believe it. Eighty-seven acres in size and nearly a mile long, Bear Island was to be his home away from home—forever!

Since the days of the American Indians, Bear Island had been inhabited. Part of it had once been farmed; stone walls zigzagged between shapeless fields. Three old houses stood on the island, the best of which became the family's home for the summer of 1905. Bucky got to know every path through the piney woods, every feature of the rocky coast. Life was rugged, but pure and clean in the most basic of ways. There was no electricity, of course (electricity existed but was rare; even the Milton house was without it). All work had to be done by hand, all food brought from the mainland ten miles away. Everyone had assigned chores. Bucky's mother, now busy with two younger children, Wolcott (Wooly) and Rosamond (Rosy), probably worked the hardest.

Even today, many lonely islands off the Maine coast do not have telephones. And in 1905, even the word *radio* was largely unknown. Communication between Bear Island and the greater world outside had to be by mail. It became Bucky's job to row the two miles to Eagle Island every day, get the mail from the mailboat that delivered there, and then row back. This was no easy task. Tides and ocean currents often made the two miles seem like five. Some days, the fog was so thick that Bucky had to use a compass.

The mail trip, as it turned out, gave Bucky an early

chance to turn a minus into a plus. It gave rise to his first useful invention. Interested in sea creatures, he had long marveled at the way a jellyfish propels itself through the water. Bending its supple body like the cupping of a hand, the jellyfish forces water out behind it as it moves along. Could such a principle be used to make rowing a boat easier? Bucky thought *yes* ... possibly. He drew a picture of what he called a "mechanical jellyfish." Then he set to work.

As Bucky later described it, his invention was a "teepee-like, folding, web-and-spirit cone which was mounted like an inside-out umbrella on the submerged end of a pole." The pole passed through a metal ring attached to the rear of the boat. When Bucky pulled on the pole, the "teepee" collapsed easily upon itself, sliding toward him through the water. Then PUSH! The cone fanned outward, "almost as though touching bottom." Bucky pushed, and the boat moved forward. He found he could "push-pole the boat along far more swiftly and easily than by sculling or rowing." An added advantage was that the operator of the boat could face forward, unlike someone rowing. Keeping a straight course shortened the trip on any day. On a foggy day, looking ahead helped avoid trouble.

Too soon for Bucky, the summer of 1905 was over, wrapped up and carried back to Milton as a memory. If he had any regrets, they concerned his relationships with the older children. Leslie was now less of a problem, but the family included two older cousins. McGregor and Andrew King had come East for the summer with Grandmother Andrews. They thought of themselves as tough westerners. Often they treated Bucky rather like a sissy. But they spent a good deal of time in another of the houses on Bear Island. Bucky had not let them ruin his summer.

Fall meant a return to Milton and to school—to spelling, to arithmetic, to "who beheaded who and who put someone in a tower," as he put it. When winter neared, however, something happened that seemed to fill the sails of summer once again with wind. Richard Fuller decided to build a huge house on Bear Island. It would be large enough to hold all the Fullers and their relatives for years to come. To draw the plans, he hired an architect named Henry Wadsworth Longfellow, Jr., a Harvard classmate and old friend. It was Longfellow who had designed the Milton house just before Bucky's birth.

The Big House—the building was called by its present name almost at once. The plans thrilled everyone. The house had two stories and an enormous dormered attic for future expansion. Porches and balconies jutted from its sides. It would sit on the highest point on Bear Island, commanding a view all around.

It was easy for the Fullers to imagine the completed house, ready and waiting for them to move in. It was not so easy, however, to figure out how the house would be constructed. Every timber, every roll of copper, every shingle, even every nail, would have to be transported to the island ten miles off the coast of Maine. Building the house would take months. The workmen would have to have a place to stay. How could all this be done?

A local contractor named Sewell agreed to do the job. To carry materials and to serve as a floating warehouse, he suggested finding an old ship. The boat could also be used as a dormitory for the workers. Finally, Sewell located the *Polly*, a creaking schooner just seaworthy enough for the job. The *Polly* had been built in 1805 and had served its country well in the War of 1812. Now this century-old ship was loaded with the materials that would become the Big House. The *Polly* left Boston about the first of June and soon lay at anchor off Bear Island.

The summer of 1906 was an important one in the development of R. Buckminster Fuller, who was later to spend years in the housing industry. Building the Big House gave him a chance to observe construction practices of the time. He watched the house go up, sill by sill, joist by joist, board by board, shingle by shingle. Longfellow's flat plans took on three-dimensional shape before his eyes.

Bucky was busy with other things as well. Grandmother Andrews bought a small motorized boat, one of the first to be seen in the area. The engine, of course, was not the efficient marine design of today. It was an old stationary-type engine that sat in the middle of the boat, as if defying forward movement with its very weight. At its best, it coughed, sputtered, and wheezed its heavy flywheel into action. At its worst—which was often—it simply refused to run. In this and future years, Bucky loved tinkering with spark plugs, gas valves, and other engine parts.

Future summers on Bear Island brought new excitement. The family purchased a much larger boat, a motorized cabin cruiser named the *Wego*. Bucky kept busy. Lumber left over from the Big House offered many temptations to a young boy with a talent for building things. Bucky built a small cabin for himself that is still in use today. When a new Victrola phonograph record player was hauled to Bear Island for the Fuller kids, Bucky designed and built a cabinet for the heavy records. It separated the thick records as they stood upright, much in the manner of the plastic-coated wire record racks that became popular years later. This cabinet, too, is still in use on Bear Island. Bucky left a lot of himself there—but probably not as much as he took away. To the end of his days, he always tried to save the month of August for still another return to the Big House...to nature, to his roots, and to the eternal sea.

When he grew older, Buckminster Fuller often looked back on the world into which he'd been born. As a child, of course, he'd simply accepted that world and his place in it. All children do, for the most part. But years later, Bucky would realize what things were like about 1900. Only 5 percent of the people had a standard of living that would be considered acceptable today. And only about 1 percent were in the very top economic and social group. Those fortunate few Bucky divided between the "wealthy" and the "comfortably off." The "wealthy" were families who not only took their servants by steamer to their Maine mansions, but also took along their prize horses and handcrafted, gilded carriages. His own family, by contrast, was just "comfortably off."

The youthful Bucky was not entirely blind to the problems of the poor. Later, as an adult he devoted most of his life to improving the lot of humanity. Even at a very young age, there must have been some sympathy in his heart. There were many poor people around him, even in the suburb of Milton. When he visited his father's bustling wharves and warehouses, he also observed the laborers whose muscle power made the whole system work. In 1965, Bucky shared a sharp memory with an audience: "When I was young, going from a little town seven miles outside of Boston into Boston through Dorchester, or Roxbury, I saw that all the children in the streets were in rags. No exceptions. People on the trolley really stank. Women of twenty-six years were hags with half their yellow teeth out. There was no dentistry for them."

But as a boy, probably, Bucky lost little sleep over the plight of the poor. He hadn't even thought about the BIG PICTURE of ailing humanity. He had his own interests and problems, just like any other child. As far as his life was concerned, he was comfortably off.

2

Teenage Troubles

Q uite early in life, R. Buckminster Fuller learned that good luck and bad luck are something like the tides. Fortunes rise for a while, then they start to fall. The main difference is that life provides no tide table. The future is always uncertain.

Grandmother Andrews, who had bought Bear Island to bring her large family together, died late in 1906. That sad event was only one sign that for Bucky the tide had turned. Another sign was that Bucky continued with troubles in school.

Those difficulties had started in the very first grade. Bucky would say something original, and the class would laugh at him. Even worse, the teacher would let him know that he was in school to learn, not to think. But Bucky had always had a lively imagination. As a four-year-old with poor eyesight, he had thought that much of what his older sister Leslie told him about the world must be made up. As a result, he had started to make up things himself. The habit continued. Before long it resulted in his teachers telling him to "shut up and learn." For the most part, Bucky obeyed the command. He really had no choice. He sat at his desk with one eye on the clock, waiting for the school day to end and his own day to begin.

At home, things were different. As an adult, Bucky would remember arriving home on his bicycle—a new-fashioned bike with wire-spoked wheels and real rubber tires! Or he would walk home through a wonderland of falling snow, to find his mother waiting with a smile and a cup of hot tea. Later, perhaps, his father would thrill the family with tales of his latest trip overseas. Why, a person could now go anywhere in the world by modern steamship! The steamer had freed travelers from schedules determined by whim of the winds. It was an exciting time to be alive. Along with Bucky's birth had come something called the wireless. This amazing invention could send messages through the air. Some experts said that there might soon be one in every living room. The first American car, too, had been built the year Bucky was born. Bucky had seen his first car at the age of seven. The Wright brothers' airplane flight near Kitty Hawk, North Carolina, in 1903 had sent American kids on a model-making binge. By the age of twelve, Bucky had built about thirty different models, biplanes and even triplanes. He sailed them out his upstairs window when he should have been doing homework.

Then quite suddenly, in 1907, tragedy struck the Fuller family.

Richard Fuller, not only Bucky's father but his idol as well, suffered a stroke—caused by damage to an artery in the brain. It was far from a "killer stroke," but it left its victim partially disabled. The successful businessman could no longer go to work. The family doctor knew of no drug that would really help. Even worse, the doctor knew of no sure way to prevent a second stroke, a possibility everyone feared. Another one could easily kill him. The medical prescription was simply rest and good care.

The whole family pitched in. A special room was fixed up for Richard Fuller, and Bucky did everything he could to help. He read aloud to the man who not long before had helped teach *him* to read. During hot summer nights, he sat fanning his father for hours. There were good days. There were bad days. But at last came what the whole family dreaded: another stroke. Then a whole series of strokes. Each left the gentle man worse off than before.

Richard Fuller was ill for three years. Toward the end of that time, in Bucky's words, "he was out of his mind. ... I had to lead my own father around by the hand, a man I loved and revered." Death finally came on July 12, 1910. It was Bucky's fifteenth birthday.

Caroline Andrews Fuller, Bucky's mother, was a deeply religious woman. But she was hardly blessed with shyness. She was strong and determined. Her first goal was to keep the family together. This was not easy, since money no longer flowed in from her husband's business. With four children to care for and feed, she had to watch every penny. All servants except the cook were let go. The Fullers would have to do the housework themselves.

Much of this work fell to the oldest son, Bucky. The experience taught him how much human energy it took to keep a house going in 1910. He had to roll up the rugs, haul them outside, and drape them over the clothesline. Then he pounded the rugs with a carpet beater. Clouds of dust filled the air. After the rugs had been carefully brushed, they were lugged back inside and rolled out on the floor.

Outside the house, Bucky had to tend the lawn and rake the driveway. Inside, he had to fill the kerosene lamps and do other chores. In the cellar squatted a stubborn monster known as a coal furnace. Bucky had to shovel coal onto the fire, shake the grates, and shovel out the ashes. Worst of all were the clinkers, masses of half-burned coal that settled into the grates and could put out the fire. These had to be poked loose, then lifted out with heavy tongs. It was hard work for a fifteen-year-old.

An important part of Mrs. Fuller's plan was to keep Bucky enrolled in a private school, Milton Academy. It was lucky that one of the leading schools in the country was located in their very town. Milton Academy was thought of as a prep school for Harvard College. Its students came from all parts of New England. Most of them, of course, came from well-to-do families who could afford the best for their sons.

Even before his father's death, Bucky had felt rather out of place at Milton. Most of the boys were boarding students. They formed a tight social knot. They were the "in" group. "There were very few of us day scholars," Bucky said later, "and you were then a little bit of a second-class kind of character...." All the A's on Bucky's report cards impressed his mother, but they made not the slightest scratch on the social system that was Milton Academy. He was still a local kid. He still went home to his mommy after sports every afternoon.

It was in sports that Bucky saw his chance. Like most normal teenagers, he wanted to be accepted. He wanted others to look up to him. And he was a good athlete. He

Bucky Fuller (lower left) on the football team.

loved testing the strength and skill of his body. He probably knew exactly what he was doing when he decided to go out for the football team.

Fuller?—on the football team? Others thought it odd. They knew that without his glasses, he could hardly tell one player from another—much less see a spot pass over center. With the small football helmets then worn, it would be impossible for him to wear glasses on the field. But when Bucky really put his mind on something, it drove ahead through the best defense. He made the team. Then he discovered that there was one position where he could control the ball and not have to see it in the air. This was the quarterback spot. He tried out for quarterback, and he made that, too. Quarterback Fuller! *Starting* Quarterback Fuller!

In later years, Fuller was often to speak of his short football career. It might be expected that his favorite memory would be a touchdown pass or a sixty-yard run. Sadly, that was not the case. The memory that cut deepest was a social one, not a moment of glory on the football field. When he first tried out for the football team, Bucky learned that the players were expected to supply their own helmets. (In those days football helmets were not the huge plastic domes players now wear. They were much smaller, head-hugging devices made of padded leather.) Now Bucky would have to ask his mother to buy a helmet. He hated to ask. She gave him no allowance, and he never had any spending money, even for important things. He had to ask his mother for everything. When he asked for the helmet, her response only made things worse. She went out and bought an inexpensive helmet herself. It wasn't even made of leather— just some kind of cheap quilting. But it was all his mother could afford. Bucky had to wear it to the first few practices. He never forgot the embarrassment.

In fact, most of Bucky's school memories centered on the social scene. He was a sensitive boy. What teachers thought of him really mattered to Bucky. What fellow students thought of him mattered even more. In *Synergetics*, his major book, he later recalled a typical experience. The teacher was busy at his or her desk. The students were supposed to be working quietly at their desks. Then some noise would come from Bucky's part of the room.

"One mark for Fuller," the teacher would say, without looking up. (A *mark* meant staying 15 minutes after school.)

Next, something would be thrown through the air.

"Two marks!"

A pause, then another noise. Again, Bucky was truly innocent. The teacher would not look up.

"Three marks for Fuller!"

And Bucky would have to stay after school, angry at his classmates and the teacher alike.

Bucky once summed up his school years in this way: "I often found myself to be the number one antifavorite amongst my schoolteachers and fellow students." But statements like this sound like the adult Fuller speaking, not the boy himself. Among Fuller's many talents was a gift for exaggeration. The best photo taken of Bucky as a schoolboy suggests quite a different picture. It shows Bucky as a member of a group, the football team. Bucky sits in the front row, ramrod straight. His just-wavy dark hair is neatly parted in the center and carefully trimmed. He wears an assured, tough-guy look on his square, handsome face. Above a strong chin, the corners of the mouth slant down a little. His muscular chest and shoulders seem to strain the fabric of his black football jersey; the only wrinkles run from side to side. He sits with his ankles crossed, his hands relaxed on his thighs. It just isn't a picture of a loner or a loser, a wimp or a washout.

Certainly, Milton Academy was far from a disaster for Bucky. He enjoyed singing in the glee club. He must have liked working in the new electrical laboratory, one of the best equipped in the country. He made some good friends, among them Lincoln Pierce, a lifelong pal. Another associate of later years was W. Starling Burgess, a Milton graduate who had made the first successful airplane flight in the Northeast. Burgess came back to the school to give an illustrated lecture about his ten-mile flight. And we know from Bucky's own account that he enjoyed science and mathematics, subjects in which he always got honors. His other grades, except for Latin, were also good. If Milton Academy was a prep school for Harvard, it did just what it was supposed to do in Bucky's case. It prepared him well. Bucky was admitted to Harvard's freshman class in 1913.

Harvard College is in Cambridge, Massachusetts, just across the Charles River from Boston. Even in Bucky's day its red-brick buildings looked old, worn with rich tradition from its founding in 1636. In contrast to busy Boston, the Harvard area was a quiet place of cool lawns and towering trees. Bucky had first heard about Harvard on his father's knee. Later, he had read the diaries that four generations of Fuller men had kept while attending Harvard. For seventeen-year-old Bucky, Havard was more than just a special place. It became a myth, a dream, a Camelot on the Charles River. For the whole Fuller family, it was unthinkable that a bright boy like Bucky should not go on to Harvard. His mother had little money, but other relatives were more than willing to help.

So in the fall of 1913, the summer tingle of Bear Island behind him, R. Buckminster Fuller entered Harvard College. He must have experienced the nervous glow that freshmen feel as they first unpack their bags in a dormitory room. It was on to a new life.

But almost at once, Bucky's dreams were attacked by cruel reality. Other Milton quarterbacks had gone on to star on the Harvard team, and Bucky had high hopes. These were dashed when he broke a kneecap during an early practice. His football career was over.

Other disappointments followed in rapid order. Bucky was a fun-loving young man. He liked nothing more than a girl on his arm, a room ringing with laughter, and the pop of champagne corks. He loved to dance. He was good at thinking up funny little poems on the spot. But once again, his dreams faded with the cold dawn of reality. His first real girlfriend left him for another man. And the Boston nightspots—only minutes away by the new subway—were beyond the reach of his bank account.

Moreover, Bucky found that he really didn't like his classes. In part, this was his own fault. At Milton Academy, he had found math and science easy. He had even taken college-level math in high school. So when the time came to choose his college classes, he decided to look at other subjects. Harder courses, he thought, would be more of a challenge. But a short time later, he found that subjects like art, music, and German literature really didn't interest him. He was bored. He started to cut classes.

Finally, Bucky's main problem again concerned the social scene. Before World War I, the social whirl at Harvard revolved around a number of clubs. Bucky learned that students' social life depended on the club they belonged to. The Porcellian Club was at the top. Its members were the real aristocrats. Other clubs formed descending rungs on the social ladder. Bucky found that his Milton friends, one by one, were being asked to join clubs. When that happened, they cut Bucky off like a social misfit. The trouble was that being asked to join a club had nothing to do with one's worth as a person. No, club membership depended on the family's wealth and social position. In fact, many club memberships were arranged by older brothers or fathers who had themselves been members of the clubs. This left Bucky in a helpless position. He had no older brother. His father was dead. And his mother had very little money.

As the first term neared its end, the sad truth became

clear. Bucky would not be asked to join a club. True, there were other freshmen who cared little about the clubs and might not have joined even if asked. But joining a club was part of the Milton-Harvard connection. More and more, Bucky felt insecure and embarrassed. He just didn't fit in. He was a marshmallow in orange juice. In this regard, his older sister Leslie was of little help. She had just married a Porcellian man and seemed to think that the club system was part of the divine order of the universe. "Bucky," she told her brother, "you're going to be a disgrace to the family. You're not going to get into any of the clubs, and all the Milton boys are."

In an interesting way, however, it was Leslie who figured in Bucky's solution to the problem. She and her husband were in the process of moving. Their huge Russian wolfhound, Mitzi, had to be left alone for a time. Would Bucky agree to walk Mitzi on a regular basis? Of course he would.

On Bucky's dog-walking rounds, he often passed a theater. Then playing was a review called the *Passing Show of 1912*. Bucky found that if he went by the stage door at just the right time, the actresses and dancers would be leaving. Mitzi was the kind of dog that everyone loves. The young women would stop to pat the dog. Bucky would answer questions, then start asking some of his own. Several of the women said yes when Bucky asked them to dinner. In this way he got dates—not just college dates, but dates with real actresses, beautiful young women! Bucky's real triumph was the yes of Marilyn Miller, breathtakingly beautiful and one of the stars of the show.

Crazy isn't the right word for it, but it's often used. A young person under pressure does something that seems

Buckminster Fuller was twice expelled from Harvard College.

completely mad. In Bucky's case, it was this: As his mid-year exams approached, the *Passing Show* moved on to New York City. Bucky went to the bank. He took out all the money his mother had deposited for his year's education. That done, he packed his best clothes and got on a train for New York. He checked into a good hotel. Then it was off to the *Passing Show*. Bucky sent Marilyn Miller roses and champagne. After the show, he went backstage. Would Marilyn Miller join him at Churchill's—then *the* place to eat in the city? She smiled and agreed. Bucky sparkled with joy. He extended the invitation to this woman, to that woman, to the whole chorus.

That night Bucky had the woman on his arm, the room full of laughter, the popping of champagne corks. As he later recalled it, "the champagne flowed like the Hudson River." The bill was staggering. So were the other bills he soon had to pay. Before long he was spending money he didn't have. The fling was over. There was only one thing to do: Go back and face Harvard—and his family.

The Harvard encounter was short, but hardly sweet. A student simply did not leave Harvard at exam time for a round of lush living. Bucky was expelled for bad conduct. That was that.

But Bucky's biggest problem lay with his family. His mother had pinched pennies for years to send him to Harvard. She had even sold the house in Milton. Her relatives felt that she had been betrayed, badly betrayed, by Bucky. She felt that way herself. A family conference was arranged. Of course, there was no way to get the money back. Whatever happened to Bucky would probably be punishment enough. But just what *would* happen to Bucky? How could he be forced to shape up?

Soon the family handed down its sentence. A cousin owned a cotton mill in Canada. The mill owner could use a strong young man like Bucky. And Sherbrooke, Quebec, was a long, long way from the bright lights of Broadway. In fact, Sherbrooke was a cold, lonely mill town that seemed to be miles away from anywhere. Bucky would earn his own money and pay his own expenses. So on a frigid day in

February 1914, Bucky packed his bags again. This time he was headed not for Harvard—nor for high living.

If punishment was part of the family's plan, it hardly seemed like that to Bucky. "I loved the people and the work," he said later. Again, a minus became a plus. Bucky's job was to help install new machinery in the cotton mill. He worked with engineers and mechanics, practical men whose ability he admired. The machines all came from overseas, from England and France. Parts were often damaged in shipment—or, in the case of the English machines, defective in the first place. The chief engineer saw Bucky's talent and put him in charge of repairing these parts. Sometimes they were so badly damaged that new parts had to be made. Bucky learned a lot about metals—one of his lifelong interests. He learned what the local metalworking shops could and could not do. He learned how to sketch diagrams for new parts of his own design. The chief engineer was more and more impressed.

Reports of Bucky's talents filtered down to Massachusetts. Why, the boy had not only mended his ways, but completely reformed! His character now seemed perfect in every way. Before many months had passed, the sentence was lifted. When Bear Island time came again, Bucky was back with his boats on the beautiful Maine coast.

To the family, a complete reformation would mean a return to Harvard. Bucky, still trying to prove himself, was willing to reapply. The Harvard authorities, too, looked at the reports from Canada. They were willing to give him another chance. Bucky became a freshman once again, this time in the entering class of 1914.

Bucky's second attempt at Harvard is less interesting than the first, but it turned out just the same. Bucky was just plain bored. He had a good memory, but he didn't like memorizing facts he saw no reason to know in the first place. Did he really want to spend four years cramming for what he considered meaningless tests? No, he decided. Once again he started to cut classes. Once again he skipped exams. It came as no surprise when he was once again expelled, again for "irresponsible conduct." Bucky had planned it just that way.

This time the family felt doubly betrayed. But Bucky was Bucky, they thought. There was no controlling him. For this reason, there was no new family plan of correction. Bucky would have to find his own way.

For a time, Bucky returned to Canada. Then he felt that old lure of New York City. He headed to New York and started looking for a job. Any kind of a job. Just as long as it paid him enough to have some fun after work. He looked all over. Wages were so low that there was hardly enough to live on. Finally he took a job as a meat handler for Armour and Company. It paid fifteen dollars a week.

Buckminster Fuller once wrote that a person's life should never be looked at as a still picture. Instead, life is like a motion picture. The individual frames run together, in constant motion. Still, it is useful to take a snapshot of Bucky's life in the spring of 1915.

Fuller men had gone to Harvard since 1740, but only Bucky had been expelled. More than that, he'd been kicked out twice. He'd betrayed the family trust. Now he worked at a job that demanded a strong back, not a quick brain. Six days a week, the job started at three in the morning. Through the echoes of nearly empty, dimly lit streets, he walked to work at an hour when the rest of the city lay asleep. Then, for twelve or fourteen hours, he lugged quarters of beef on and off trucks, down into the dark holds of ships, or into central markets. It was dirty work, sheer drudgery. Bucky's fellow workers were hardly the Porcellians of Harvard Yard. Once "comfortably off," he had now grasped at the social ladder, missed, and fallen off. He had come down in the world.

If there was one comforting thought in Bucky's mind at the time, it could have been this: You can't fall off the floor.

3

"The Time of My Life"

In 1965, at the height of his fame, R. Buckminster Fuller shared a memory with an eager audience. The story he told may have been made up, or partly made up. But that is really beside the point. The point is the *point* of the story. Fuller sometimes used stories to illustrate a more important truth than the truth of what really happened. The BIG PICTURE again.

The happening occurred in 1913, just before Bucky went off to Harvard. A rich uncle took him aside for a man-to-man talk. "Young man," the uncle said, "I think I must tell you some things that won't make you very happy. I know that you are impressed with your grandmother's golden rule: 'do unto others as you would they should do unto you.'" But that wasn't the way the real world worked. No, the uncle went on, "the golden rule doesn't work. Those few of us who are rich and who really have the figures know that it is worse than one chance in one hundred that you can survive your allotted days in any comfort. It is not you or the other fellow; it is you or one hundred others." Putting it differently, for a family of five to be "comfortably off," five hundred others had to suffer. To survive, you had to be a winner, to triumph over others, said the uncle. "So do it as neatly and as cleanly and politely as you know how and as your conscience will allow."

So, it was a dog-eat-dog world! Worse than that, even. It was a world ruled by the male dogs. Part of a top dog's responsibility was to shelter the fragile females from the truth. The ladies had to be protected in their innocent, golden-rule happiness. The uncle felt quite proud that he had taken care of the grandmother's "hundred others"— without her even knowing about it.

Bucky's meat-carrying job in New York put him in quick touch with the "others" of the world. He found that he could get along fine with most of the men he worked with. He admired their strength. He wondered at their ability to keep going, day after day. But that was all. Most of them had had only a few years of school, if any. "My fellow workman was intellectually timid to a fault," Bucky said later. "He was a slave; he knew he had very little chance of happy and healthy survival. He was afraid of his words and his mind. He communicated his feelings by the way he chewed to-bacco, spat, and blasphemed [swore], using a total vocabulary of no more than about fifty words."

Clearly, Bucky was quite different from his fellow workers. He had more than fifty words in his mind—a lot more. This difference was soon noticed by his bosses. They moved him up to a cashier's job. They gave him a small raise in pay. Then they made Bucky what today might be called a "management trainee." To give him experience, they moved him around from place to place in New York and New Jersey. In less than two years, Bucky worked at twenty-eight branches of Armour and Company. This gave him the BIG PICTURE of the company's business. He learned that meat went bad fast. It had to be distributed quickly, cleanly, and efficiently. Thus Bucky got his first lessons in distribution patterns. He certainly never imagined that he would later become an expert in distribution patterns for all the earth's resources, the world around.

In other ways, too, Bucky's life began to look up. He still loved the bright lights. His amazing energy allowed him to dance into the night, get a few hours sleep, and go to work fresh and ready for another long workday. Of course, his social life took money. But here again he was lucky. His mother, who no longer owned the Milton house, came to New York. She rented a Manhattan apartment. Bucky had hardly been cast out by the family. Now his mother did what she could to bring him a home away from home.

Caroline Fuller had another good reason to move to New York. She wanted to be close to her oldest child, now Leslie Larned. Leslie had married well. Her husband was the rich and athletic sportsman, Edward P. Larned. They lived where they wanted to live, and they mingled with the best. For the summer of 1915, they rented a house in Lawrence, Long Island. Lawrence was a wealthy community on the Atlantic coast. Mrs. Fuller often traveled to Lawrence to spend time with Leslie and some friends. Before long, when Bucky had a free weekend, he also made the short trip to Lawrence.

Bucky soon made friends among the well-to-do Lawrence young people. One Saturday night a friend, Tilden

Hazard, wangled him an invitation to a dance. The party was held in a private house, one of the many stately homes in Lawrence that could host such an affair. The large rooms glittered in splendor. The live music spilled out through open windows and spiraled upward toward the July stars. It was a formal event. The men wore tuxedos. The women wore elegant dresses with long, swirling skirts.

It was the women, of course, that Bucky looked over first. One woman, in particular, caught his eye—as she did the attention of all twenty or so men present. Her name was Anx Hewlett (really Anglesea, but nobody called her that). Only fifteen years old, she had long golden hair, stunning blue eyes, and a face that caused hearts to skip a few beats, if not melt. She was also something of a flirt. Bucky thanked friendly fortune when he finally got to dance with her. He also danced with Anx's sister, a beautiful brunette named Anne. She was almost as pretty as her sister Anx, but in a different way. Anne had roses on her cheeks and large, captivating brown eyes. She also seemed more mature than her sister Anx. Bucky, who had just turned twenty, learned that Anne was nineteen.

The next day another friend, Ken Phillips, suggested that he and Bucky pay a call on the Hewlett sisters. Bucky didn't need to be asked twice. Before long they presented themselves at the Hewletts' door at the end of Martin's Lane. The visit had been Phillips's idea, so Bucky let him take the lead. It was soon clear that Phillips's real interest was in Anne, not in Anx. Bucky didn't mind at all. He knew neither young woman well. After all, Anx was the one with the cover-girl face and figure. Even more important, the four seemed to hit it off at once. They had fun together.

That was Bucky's first visit to the large brick and shingle

house where, over the years, he would spend a lot of time. During the summer of 1915, he went to Leslie's every weekend he could. From there it was only a short walk to the Hewletts'. It was Ken Phillips and Anne, Bucky and Anx. Double dating was common then, and the foursome seemed to belong together. It might seem there wasn't much to do on a date. A new invention, the silent motion picture, was about the hottest thing in the area. A "date" was usually a visit—sandwiches in the dining room or lemonade on the lawn. It was considered rather daring when they sailed out to an island for a picnic.

The Hewlett household was a strange and wonderful one. Children were everywhere. Anne, the oldest of ten, was definitely no longer a child. She was often forced by her position to be more like a mother. Mrs. Hewlett was an invalid who spent most of her time in an upstairs room. The father, James Monroe Hewlett, was a well-known painter and architect. He was a gentle, caring man, but his work often kept him away. Anne had to help manage the servants and the kids. Most of the children were headstrong, fun-loving, even wild. Anne herself was a fun-loving person, but she did her best to take care of the others. Something was always happening at the Hewlett house. Any excuse would do for a party. The kids loved to write and put on little plays. At best, they were talented children who tried to cooperate without a parent on the scene. At worst, they fought like crazy. Bucky himself, strong as he was, hesitated to step into the battles.

Two things began to worry Bucky as the summer neared its end. First, he felt himself growing more fond of Anne and less attracted to the dazzling Anx. Yet Anne was supposed to be Ken Phillips's girl, and Phillips was his good friend. There were rumors, even, that Anne and Ken were secretly engaged. The whole situation was one big problem. Second, the end of the summer meant that he might never see either of the sisters again. When fall came, the Hewletts would return to their winter home in Brooklyn. A weekend trip to Leslie's could no longer really be a visit to the Hewlett's.

Unknown to Bucky, it was Anne who would put an end to both these worries. The fall season had hardly started when she invited Bucky to dinner in Brooklyn. The whole family liked Bucky's good humor, and he was genuinely fond of both Anne's parents. Bucky said yes to the invitation. Again he had a good time at the Hewletts', and again he was invited to dinner. More invitations followed. But because of his friendship with Ken, Bucky tended to act formal and shy with Anne. It was she who broke the ice that was already melting between them. She came right out and said it: Certainly, she was not engaged to Kenneth Phillips. Bucky should forget any attachment he imagined between them. In other words, Bucky was free to court Anne himself.

Back in 1915, courting was rather formal. The word *date* today hardly means an evening-long visit with a girl's family. But in Bucky's youth, it often did. Not that he dreaded the idea at first. He liked Mrs. Hewlett, and he rather enjoyed the long visits at her bedside upstairs. As for Mr. Hewlett, Bucky had nothing but admiration. The kind and talented James Monroe Hewlett was a gifted man. He designed and painted sets for top Broadway shows. He designed houses. He constantly studied new building materials and methods of construction. These activities fascinated Bucky. What Bucky didn't like was the part the other Hewlett children chose to play in his courtship.

Anne Hewlett about 1915.

Anything the Hewletts did, they did in a big way. When they squabbled, they fought tooth and nail. And when they teased, it was torture. Bucky was used to their constant teasing. They teased each other at every chance, and to be a Hewlett friend meant to be teased as well. But Bucky never expected the kids' reaction when they saw the stars come out in the lovers' eyes. Although the Brooklyn house had many rooms, it was almost impossible for Bucky and Anne to find a moment alone. A door was always opening, or some "emergency" would demand Anne's attention. Because Bucky worked for a huge meat-packing company, he was called "the butcher boy." Sometimes the kids would get together and chant at the top of their lungs:

Listen! Listen! Listen!
Anne and Bucky kissin'.
Where? Where? Where?
In the big, red chair.
How? How? How?
     WOW!

With the last loud syllable, the kids would explode with laughter.

Bucky, however, refused to give up. Anne loved roses, and he loved sending them. For several weeks he spent a third of his pay at a florist shop near the Fulton Market in lower Manhattan. As the winter wore on, it became clear to all that Anne and Bucky were, indeed, really serious about each other. It also became clear that the frisky little Hewletts were the least of their problems.

Old Daniel Willetts lived near the Hewletts in Brooklyn. He was Anne's grandfather, on her mother's side. He had loved Anne dearly from the day she was born. A successful businessman, he had showered Anne with gifts. He had even taken her on trips to Europe. Now he learned that his precious Anne was in love. With whom? With a college drop-out, a high-spirited nobody. Why, Bucky had never earned a decent day's pay in his life. How did he think he could support a wife? Especially a well-bred young woman who was used to the best.

Grandfather Willetts's feelings must have meant a lot to Anne. She tried to break it off with Bucky, which made him miserable. She felt miserable herself. She couldn't keep up the act. Before long, Daniel Willetts saw that the Fuller boy was coming around again, looking happier than ever. Noticing this, the old man threw up another barrier. It suddenly developed that Anne's great-aunt Kate had a desperate need to see California, even parts of western Canada such as Lake Louise, over two thousand miles away. She needed a companion to go along on the trip. Would Anne go? The family decided that Anne would have to go.

But the trip did not go as Grandfather Willetts had planned. In this case, absence really did make the heart grow fonder. Anne got off the last train home more in love with Bucky than ever. She told Bucky she would marry him. Days later, her parents blessed the union. The engagement was announced, and the young people of Lawrence had another reason to throw party after party.

No date could be set for the wedding. Bucky was no longer a "butcher boy," but his paycheck was still a small one. His wishes alone couldn't support a wife in a comfortable apartment. If he worked hard at Armour and Company, he thought, the day might not be too far off. But another day, as well, might not be too far off. That was the day the United States would finally be forced to enter World War I.

The trouble had started three years earlier, deep in eastern Europe. Almost unnoticed in the United States, a dispute between two small nations had become violent. Then, one by one, the great powers of Europe had entered the conflict. Now Germany, Austria-Hungary, and Turkey faced France, Britain, and Russia. The United States had tried to keep out of the war, but the effort met with less and less success. In 1915 a German submarine had sunk the British passenger liner *Lusitania*, killing over a thousand people, including 128 Americans. President Woodrow Wilson, continuing to plead for peace, had asked for a buildup in the army and navy. Most Americans, partly because of the *Lusitania*, felt themselves on the side of Britain and France.

President Wilson's plan to keep out of the war depended on one thing: The Germans would have to observe the old doctrine of freedom of the seas. The United States was a neutral nation. Officially it had not taken sides in the war. Its ships carrying material to Britain and France were not supposed to be attacked by German U-boats, or submarines.

For years the Germans had promised not to attack American shipping. For years they had kept that pledge. Then quite suddenly, early in 1917, the German war plan changed. The Germans announced they would shoot at any ships heading for British or French ports. This was too much for most Americans to take. This meant war.

No one really liked sending young men off into battle on foreign soil, but most people agreed that it had to be done. Bands played everywhere. Song writers forgot about the moon in June and turned to "Over There" and "When the Boys Come Marching Home." Older women volunteered to roll bandages and sell Liberty Bonds. Younger women tried to do the work of their departing husbands. Millions of young American men were eager to sign up in the army or navy.

R. Buckminster Fuller, of course, was caught up in the war fever that swept the country. Engaged to Anne or not, he had to do his part. With his knowledge of boats and love for the sea, he chose the navy. He hurried to the navy's recruiting station in New York—only to fail the eye examination. He even tried to cheat, but the examiners were on the lookout for that. They spotted him at once.

As it turned out, that minus became another plus. With war on the horizon, the whole Atlantic coast became a target for German U-boats. The danger was clear. German submarines could sail into any big harbor, then shoot at anything. On lonely beaches, the Germans could land spies, even secret agents armed with explosives to blow up key targets. Officials in Washington knew that the Atlantic coast had to be protected at any cost.

So did Bucky. Knowing that coastal patrol boats were needed, he thought of the *Wego*. The family's old cabin cruiser on Penobscot Bay might not be navy gray, but it might be needed. Mrs. Fuller, after some persuasion, agreed to let the *Wego* go to war. Bucky got in touch with his old Milton friend, Lincoln Pierce. "Linc" liked the idea, and together they went up to Bear Island. Their hands froze as they polished the *Wego* to a military shine. They teased the old motor to its patriotic best. Finally, they headed the *Wego* toward nearby Bar Harbor, the nearest naval station on the Maine coast. Would the navy accept *Wego*? Would the navy also accept its crew?

To this day, no one knows how or why young Bucky Fuller was accepted by the U.S. Navy. His bad eyes would have failed him at any regular recruiting station. He had already proved that in New York. Yet in Bar Harbor, Maine, the officials probably looked only at the *Wego*. Patrol boats were desperately needed, and the men who came with them had to be taken, too. Bucky was offered the rank of chief boatswain. This really surprised him. At the time, chief boatswain was the highest enlisted man's rank in the navy. It would allow him to wear a white officer's uniform, even the impressive billed cap that no ordinary sailor could wear.

Linc Pierce became second in command, and other crew members were signed up. The *Wego*, docked in Bar Harbor, put to sea on a regular schedule. On calm days, it was easy to scan the waters for the rising periscopes of enemy submarines. But in stormy weather, with visibility limited, it was all the crew could do to keep the little *Wego* safely afloat. Only forty feet long, the cabin cruiser hadn't really been built for all-weather service on the open sea.

The crew of the *Wego* never spotted any U-boats, but they did perform an important service. One night they put in for repairs near Machias, an isolated town on the northern coast. They noticed some signal lights flashing between the mainland and an offshore island. The lights seemed to be communicating in some sort of secret code. Then a big fishing boat, as if by signal, began churning its way out to the island. His suspicions aroused, Bucky reported all he had seen as soon as possible. The navy investigated at once. It was found that a large sardine-packing factory, along with the boats that served it, had been equipped as a refueling station for German submarines. The factory had recently been purchased by a businessman. Some of his so-called diesel tanks really held fuel for German subs. His fishing boats could go where they wanted without attracting attention, even at night. What looked like a perfect operation was put out of business by the crew of the little *Wego*.

Other excitement followed. As a chief boatswain, Bucky's navy salary was $1,800 a year. This was good money for 1917. It was twice what he had earned at Armour and Company. Now, perhaps, he could finally marry Anne Hewlett. She had the same idea. Remembering that Bucky's father had died on Bucky's fifteenth birthday, she suggested a happier event for the twelfth day of July. Bucky and his *Wego* friends arranged a short leave from the navy. Back in Lawrence, Anne arranged for the wedding. It would be held at Rock Hall, her grandmother's huge white mansion. Rock Hall was—and still is—one of the finest old homes on the Long Island coast.

The wedding was a high point in Fuller's life. First, it was held on the Rock Hall lawn. A movie director, searching the Atlantic coast for a splashy wedding scene, might not have found a better spot. Also, it let Bucky know that he was no longer the "black sheep" of the family. The Fullers were there, with all the relatives. The Hewletts were also there, with all their relatives. Bucky felt honored. Handsome and trim in his tailored navy whites, he looked as glowing as Anne in her low-cut, full-skirted gown. Linc Pierce, also in uniform, was the best man. Anx, dazzling as always, served as maid of honor. The many uniforms provided a patriotic tone. The festivities ended with Bucky and Anne's dashing under an archway formed by sparkling swords.

There could be no honeymoon trip, for Fuller had to report back for *Wego* service. What honeymoon there was took place at the little Bar Harbor cottage that Fuller had rented. It was an odd honeymoon in another way as well. Bucky always loved to have a lot of people around. He and Anne asked Linc Pierce and Anx to join then for a few days.

Another couple accepted their invitation as well. The wedding party went on, right into the honeymoon.

The Bar Harbor cottage was the first of many homes Bucky and Anne were to share. The next few were not homes, really—more like navy quarters or hotel rooms. As long as the war lasted, Anne tried to follow Bucky from station to station. She usually succeeded. They were together as much as possible.

After the formal declaration of war in April 1917, many other small boats had been offered to the navy for patrol duty. Nearly all of them were better than the small *Wego*. As the Maine fleet grew larger, the old *Wego* found itself outclassed. With a top speed of eight knots, it literally could not keep up. Fuller was not surprised when the *Wego* was retired. What did surprise him was the series of opportunities that lay ahead.

Fuller was given command of the *Inca*, a nearly new cruiser. The *Inca* was seventy-two feet long. It could do twenty-eight knots. Because of the *Inca's* amazing speed, it was sent to serve as a rescue ship at the U.S. Navy flight-training school in Virginia. The flying school needed rescue ships because of the poor design of the early seaplanes. Naval aviation was just beginning. The first planes, which were really land planes equipped with pontoons, tended to nose over if they hit the sea at too steep an angle. When this happened, the pilot was suddenly under water. He was left hanging upside down by his seatbelt in an open cockpit. Fast rescue ships tried to speed to the disaster in time. Trained divers hurled themselves from the decks of ships like the *Inca*. They would then try to free the pilot before he drowned. Often it would be too late. A bad landing usually meant death.

Bucky Fuller had a better idea. Why not try to lift the

whole plane out of the water? Wouldn't this be better than sending divers to grope below? Fuller designed a mast and boom to be installed on the stern of a ship. A hook would be quickly attached to the overturned plane. This hook, hanging from the boom and attached by cable to a fast winch, would pull the plane upward. Fuller took his drawings to his superior, Commander Pat Bellinger. Yes, said Bellinger. Go ahead. Try it. It might work.

Fuller's idea not only worked, it worked well. Soon all the *Inca*'s sister ships were equipped with Fuller's boom. Because of it, the navy saved many lives that would otherwise have been lost to the sea.

From that point on, Commander Bellinger had his eye on Chief Boatswain Fuller. Here, he thought, was a young man with promise. Soon another opportunity came along. Naval aviation clearly had a future, but at first there were many problems. One of these was the lack of communication between ships and planes in the air. In 1907, a scientist named Lee De Forest had invented a radio tube that allowed voice transmission for the first time. Dr. De Forest was now working on a project that would put ships in voice contact with the planes above them. A reliable ship was needed for the final test. Commander Bellinger gave the job to Fuller and the *Inca*.

Fuller enjoyed working with the famous scientist. As De Forest brought his equipment on board and got it ready, Fuller learned all he could. Radio communication was an exciting new science. De Forest seemed glad to teach the eager young man all he knew. Finally, the day came for the big test. It went well. It was on Fuller's ship, the cruiser *Inca*, that sea and sky said hello for the first time in history.

Commander Bellinger had even more good news in

store for Fuller. At the time, the navy had a desperate need for officers. The old United States Naval Academy at Annapolis had always been run like a four-year college. It couldn't possibly turn out all the officers the war required. For this reason, an emergency program was started. Outstanding enlisted men who had been to college and served overseas were offered a special chance. First they would have to get through a very hard, ninety-day cram course at Annapolis. Then they would be allowed to take the examination to become officers in the United States Navy.

Fuller was accepted into the program—though how he did it remains something of a mystery. He did not have the required college education. He had not yet served overseas. And his eyes—they didn't qualify him for the navy's lowest rank. Probably, Commander Bellinger pulled some strings. He was a highly respected career officer and he knew the right people. If he said young Fuller must be a navy officer, that was that.

Bellinger was right about young Fuller. At the Naval Academy, Bucky Fuller had to compete against the very best. His classmates had been top students in their college graduating classes. Fuller had even known some of them at Harvard. Years later, Fuller said that he never worked harder in his life than during those three months. Anne moved into a nearby hotel, but Bucky could find little time to spend with her. There was so much to learn. Mathematics, engineering, even law. Detail after detail about ships, naval maneuvers, and command. Finally, after three months of unending mental toil, the sleepless Chief Boatswain Fuller graduated near the top of his class. He was a "ninety-day wonder." He was now Ensign Fuller and would soon be a lieutenant.

The Naval Academy gave Fuller a new respect for

himself and also for the United States Navy. The Harvard castoff had now proved himself as a top student. In fact, some Harvard men had failed the crash program. And Fuller now admired the navy more than ever. The navy's scope of operations was not just the Maine coast or even the whole United States. No, the navy's interest was the seven seas, the whole world, the BIG PICTURE. Also, the navy kept up with the cutting edge of scientific advance. At last, Fuller had found his true calling: the United States Navy.

After graduation, Fuller was assigned to the staff of Admiral Albert Gleaves. Operating out of New Jersey, Gleaves's office managed the entire troop-transport operation to Europe. Once again, Fuller's ability was recognized. He was made a special assistant to the admiral. Part of Fuller's job was to keep track of where each of 130 ships was at any given time. His scope was the whole Atlantic Ocean. Then, in October 1918, Fuller was sent to find out what life on a troop transport was really like. He found himself assigned to one of the transport ships, the *Great Northern*. Soon Fuller's ship sailed off on a trip to France. On the return voyage, the great news finally came: The Germans had surrendered. The war was over!

Fortunately for Bucky, the *Great Northern* returned in time for him to be on hand for a special event. On December 12, 1918, Anne gave birth to a baby girl. They named her Alexandra. As Bucky looked down at the small, frail body, he must have felt a special thrill. He was now a happily married man and the father of a lovely child. He had a new career that he loved—the United States Navy. As he himself said later, the time was a good one, "the time of my life."

CHAPTER

4

Frowns of Fortune

A ll experts on R. Buckminster Fuller agree on one thing: Any biography of Bucky must say a lot about his wife, Anne.

Throughout their long marriage, Bucky dashed from this idea to that, this project to that, this place to that. His inner force led outward, spiraling into space. It was Anne who pulled things back together. The two were opposites in many ways. But in fact, these opposing forces often led to balance and peace. Near the end of his life, Fuller was to say this:

"When two people as diametrically [totally] different as Anne and I get married, it either cracks up right away, or it turns out to be fantastically good—the way it has been for us."

A good friend of the Fullers said that the right words to describe Anne are *strength, beauty,* and *grace.* Notice the order of those words. It must have taken a lot of strength to stick with Bucky at times. The marriage had its full share of rocky spots. Bucky's life was Bucky's show. He could be hard to get along with. It took a strong and sensible person to stay in the background, to let Bucky be Bucky. Anne had the deep inner strength to take a lifelong risk on the man she loved.

During the first year and a half of their marriage, Bucky hopped from success to success in the navy. Anne followed him from place to place, patiently waiting, there for support when he needed it. As she was giving birth to his child, Bucky was deciding on a navy career that would take them from place to place for years. That was the lucky case: shore duty. Duty at sea would leave her alone for weeks or months at a time.

As it happened, sea duty came first. Anne stayed at her parents' home with baby Alexandra while Bucky went off again. It was another of his great assignments. He was made a communications officer on the battleship *George Washington*. The ship was already one of the navy's best, and now it was being painted and polished for a very special duty. President Woodrow Wilson wanted to make sure that American men had not died in vain. He wanted no more wars. He wanted to see a world where democracy was safe, for everyone, forevermore. He announced that he would attend the Paris Peace Conference himself. No other American president had ever traveled to Europe, but Woodrow Wilson was a determined man. He wanted to do all he could to shape the future of a new kind of world. The name of the ship that carried him to France was a fitting one: the *George Washington*.

As the ship was made ready for President and Mrs. Wilson, Bucky Fuller got to meet an old friend. Dr. Lee De Forest came aboard to install state-of-the-art radio equipment. The two men had worked together before, on the cruiser *Inca*, proving that ship-to-plane voice contact was possible. De Forest's new equipment promised even more of a breakthrough. Before the presidential voyage, ship-to-shore radio range was limited to seventy miles or so. De Forest now wanted to prove that a president of the United States could cross the Atlantic and remain in instant touch with Washington, D.C.

The trip to France, with the presidential party on board, went as smoothly as planned. As a communications officer, Fuller kept busy with De Forest's complicated equipment. There is no record that a minor navy officer named Fuller ever got to dine with Woodrow Wilson. But Bucky Fuller was right there when the ship docked at Brest, a harbor on the French coast. President Wilson picked up a telephone and spoke into it. His words were heard at a special receiving station in Alexandria, Virginia. That fact was bigger news than whatever Wilson happened to say.

Fuller was to serve on a second presidential crossing, another happy experience. Meanwhile, back on Long Island, all was far from happy. Bucky's visits home were marred by misfortune. Tiny Alexandra Fuller fell victim to the great influenza epidemic of 1918–19.

Today, the term *World War I* means something to most Americans. People think of troops in sodden trenches, of gas attacks and gas masks, of biplanes dueling in the sky in the best Red Baron style. Not so well remembered, however, is the great flu epidemic that happened near the end of the war. Influenza was the real killer of the war years. For every U.S. soldier who died on a French battlefield, ten Americans at home fell victim to the flu. Medical science could do little. Flu shots were unheard of. The deadly new kind of flu struck late in 1918 and swept across countries around the world and reached the United States. Nearly every family was touched in some way. Before the epidemic was over, the disease killed about 21 million people around the world. In the United States more than half a million Americans lay dead.

Fortunately, little Alexandra Fuller did not die. But for a time it was close. She teetered between life and death. The infant was a beautiful child, but she had always been small and fragile. Alexandra survived, but she never totally recovered. The flu weakened her, leaving her at the mercy of other childhood diseases of the time.

Bucky and Anne had always been devoted to their baby. Now, with Alexandra's illness, that devotion became total. Bucky learned that his next navy assignment would take him to the Philippines. Admiral Gleaves, for whom Bucky had worked during the war, had put in a special request. Gleaves wanted Fuller as his assistant on a long tour of duty in the Pacific. But could Bucky go? With Anne alone, he would not have hesitated. Navy wives were used to following their husbands to the far reaches of the seven seas. But could Bucky take a sick child like Alexandra to a place like the Philippines? He decided he couldn't. He could not desert his daughter. He loved the navy with a passion, but he loved his family more. His family came first now that the war was over.

On August 28, 1919, Lieutenant Richard Buckminster Fuller resigned from active service in the United States Navy.

Now Bucky was a civilian, and he had to find a job. At the time, prospects were not very good. Peace had been declared in Europe, but the nation had not yet returned to a peaceful life. Unemployment was high. News of labor unrest—strikes and even violence—filled the papers. Before the war, Bucky had started to climb the ladder at Armour and Company. Now he went back to the meat-packing company and asked about a job. The top people at Armour remembered Bucky. They were impressed with his war record. They offered him the position of assistant export manager. The salary was fifty dollars a week.

In the days when a nickel bought a big candy bar or a subway ride, fifty dollars a week was not at all bad. Bucky took the job. It taught him more about distribution patterns, this time patterns around the world. The job also allowed him to move his small family out of his in-laws' home. The young Fullers rented an inexpensive little house on Pearsal Place in Lawrence. Bucky, after hours, worked with lumber and paint to fix up the outside of the house. Anne made the inside look its very best.

Alexandra, however, remained a concern. After the influenza attack, she fell ill with another disease. Spinal meningitis killed a lot of children who caught it, but again Alexandra survived. Then she got infantile paralysis, also known as polio. It left little Alexandra unable to walk.

Alexandra's long struggle with disease cost the Fullers a lot of money. Anne and Bucky insisted on the best medical care. At times the child needed around-the-clock nursing. This was more than the parents could handle alone. Bucky's fifty dollars a week could not possibly cover two nurses, along with the usual bills. Caroline Fuller, and later Anne's parents, had to help out with the bills. Moving expenses also added to the problems. The Pearsal Place house proved drafty and hard to heat in the winter. For a time Bucky and Anne tried a small apartment on Montague Street in Brooklyn. That wasn't much better. In the summer of 1921, loaded with bills and constantly worried about Alexandra, they moved back into the Hewletts' big house at the end of Martin's Lane in Lawrence.

Bucky was worried that Alexandra might not make it through another cold, damp winter. Through a business connection, he found that he could rent a little house in Bermuda for very little money. Anne and Alexandra left for the warmer climate. They had a good winter. Anne's sister Anx went with them, and friends visited from time to time. When they returned in the spring, Bucky was overjoyed. Little Alexandra could not only stand up by herself, she could walk! She could even run around a little.

Alexandra's health was not the only good news for Bucky. About that time, a friend of his was made president of the Kelly-Springfield Truck Company. Would Fuller be interested in a position as national sales manager? At a good raise in pay? Of course he would! Fuller left Armour and joined Kelly-Springfield. He threw his talent and energy into the job. He did well. Kelly-Springfield's sales started to climb.

At home, Bucky continued to be thrilled with Alexandra's progress. Both parents noticed that the cute little tot seemed to have unusual ability. The parents would be talking about something. Bucky would have a thought in his mind, but before he could say it, Alexandra would come out with the words. She seemed to be able to read people's minds. For Bucky, Alexandra's gift couldn't be called unnatural. Since it was a fact, it had to be natural in some way. There had to be a natural explanation. Scientists were then finding new kinds of radio waves. Couldn't some very short waves, as yet undiscovered, explain how his unspoken thought could enter Alexandra's mind? This led to Bucky's

lifelong interest in telepathy, or silent communication between minds. He was sure that it was a perfectly natural
ability—and that some people were better at it than others.

Telepathy, however, didn't let Fuller know what was in
store for him at work. He suddenly lost his job at Kelly-
Springfield. The whole truck company was to go out of
business. Period. There was nothing anybody could do about
it. What particularly bothered Fuller was learning that the
decision had been made months before. People on high
levels of finance and business had made plans to close Kelly-
Springfield even before he and his friend were hired. He
had worked hard for three months and even increased sales.
But for what? It was a deliberate and dirty double cross. This
was one of several experiences that led to Fuller's increasing
dislike of bankers and businessmen.

From 1920 into 1922, the whole country was going
through a severe business slump. Many people lost their
jobs. Unemployed and betrayed, Fuller was depressed. His
usually high spirits went down and down. He started
drinking. Fuller had always been glad to lift another glass at
a party, but he had never before been a serious drinker. In
an effort to escape the blues, he signed up for summer duty
with the navy. He was still a reserve officer, and as such was
offered command of a small training ship, the *Eagle Boat 15*.
The boat was neither big nor graceful, and the job wouldn't
last long. But it was something to do, and it paid a little
money.

Once on board, Fuller felt much better. The salt spray
was again on his face, and he could feel the roll of the waves.
Moreover, the navy had paired him up with another reserve
officer he liked at once. Vincent Astor came from one of the
richest families in America. He had inherited $70 million on

his twenty-first birthday. Yet he and penniless Fuller were soon the best of buddies. Among its stops, the *Eagle Boat 15* went to Newport, Rhode Island. Newport was a summer gathering place for the rich and super-rich. Astor knew everybody worth knowing, and he led Fuller through the social whirl.

Vincent Astor owned a seaplane. It was probably the most advanced flying ship in the nation. A high-winged monoplane with a pusher prop, it landed on a boatlike hull, not on pontoons. Fuller thought it a masterpiece of technology. He loved its sleek lines. Astor employed a pilot, but Fuller sometimes got to control the plane once it was aloft. When not in use, the plane was usually kept not far from the Hewletts' Long Island home.

The summer over, Fuller received a pleasant surprise. Vincent Astor said he had to go to Europe on business. Why didn't Bucky and Anne use the plane while he was away? The pilot had been paid through October. Fuller wouldn't even have to buy fuel. Astor claimed that the plane needed use. The Fullers couldn't resist the offer. In September, they took a rare vacation. Alexandra was well enough to leave behind, with the Hewletts and a nurse. Stopping here and there on the way, they flew to Bear Island. Everywhere they went, the plane drew crowds of people. Newspapers carried pictures of the plane—and the seemingly wealthy young couple it carried. It was fun while it lasted.

Back at home, however, things went no better. Fuller remained unemployed and unhappy. October passed slowly, with Fuller again drinking too much. In November, a friend invited him to the Yale-Harvard football game. It was to be played at Harvard that year. Fuller would have a chance to see some old friends in the Boston area. And surely, he needed a change of scene. He accepted.

At the time, Alexandra, now nearly four, seemed to be doing well. She was healthy enough to walk the short distance to the Lawrence station with Bucky and Anne. As they strolled along, Bucky carried a cane. Canes were in fashion that year, and his old football knee gave him an excuse to use one. The cane reminded Bucky of the smaller canes he would see at the football game. He told Alexandra about the little canes to which college pennants were attached. He decribed the stadium scene he was soon to see: thousands of people would be waving pennants on little canes as they filled the air with cheers.

Alexandra seemed interested. She looked up at her father. "Daddy, will you bring me a cane?"

Fuller promised that he would. Soon he was on the train, then on another train headed for Boston. It was a good football game. Harvard won. Afterward, Fuller went out with some friends to celebrate the victory. Throughout the long evening, the liquor flowed freely. (Prohibition—no-alcohol—laws had gone into effect, but they were often ignored. Party-minded people like Fuller's friends knew where to go to get illegal alcohol and had the money.) Fuller and his drinking buddies honored dear old Harvard with full alcoholic respect.

The next afternoon Bucky's homeward train finally arrived in New York City. He went at once to a telephone booth, to say hi to Anne. Her news shocked him. Not long after his departure, Alexandra had developed a fever. The doctor, called at once, had diagnosed the illness as pneumonia. Now, Anne said, Alexandra was in a coma, unconscious. Of course Bucky caught the first train to Lawrence and dashed to Martin's Lane.

Alexandra was still in a coma. Her condition didn't change during the evening. Anne, Bucky, and the doctor hovered over her, helpless but hopeful. After all, Alexandra had pulled through crises before. Midnight came. The child seemed now a little better, now a little worse. During one of her better moments, she opened her eyes and looked up. There was Bucky.

"Daddy," Alexandra asked in a thin little voice, "did you bring me my cane?"

Bucky was speechless. He had forgotten all about the cane. Busy with friends and drunk with more than joy, he hadn't remembered his promise.

A few hours later, Alexandra Fuller died in her heart-broken father's arms. The tears in his eyes would come again for years.

5

Stockade and Solitude

Alexandra's death left her parents with an aching sense of loss. Another light in Bucky's world had gone dark. He wanted to strike out at Death somehow, to fight back. Some of his anger was directed at the medical profession. This was supposed to be the new age of science. Signs of progress were everywhere. Why hadn't doctors done something about the four diseases that had weakened and finally killed his lovely child?

It made things worse that most people didn't even expect to see cures for these diseases. People just thought that nothing could be done. "Nobody even tried to do anything about them," Fuller said later. It was the same way with housing. Fuller felt sure that poor housing had contributed to Alexandra's death. He blamed faulty sanitation, cold drafts, and stuffy rooms.

But most of all, Fuller blamed himself. He felt that he

could—and should—have done more to prevent the tragedy. After all, what had he really done? At the age of twenty-seven, he was unemployed. He hadn't provided his family with a clean, healthful place to live. He'd spent too much money on alcohol. He'd avoided his duties in the pursuit of selfish pleasures. Where had he been when Alexandra fell ill for the last time? Out having a good time with friends.

"A winter of horror"—that was how Bucky described the period that followed. Anne's mother, long an invalid, passed away not long after Alexandra. This meant that Anne had to take on more duties in the Martin's Lane house. She had to care for her younger sisters and brothers. Bucky remained without a job. He couldn't seem to escape the pain that followed him everywhere.

It was Anne's father who finally brought some relief.

James Monroe Hewlett had invented a new kind of building block. It was the size of the standard concrete block that is still used today, except that it was only half as high. What made it unique was its composition. Hewlett had mixed straw and cement together to make a much lighter block. His blocks were strong enough for most building uses. They were also easier to handle and cheaper to make. They were fireproof and waterproof.

Hewlett had been able to patent his idea. That meant he had registered his idea and design with the government. A patent is a government document giving the inventor rights to the invention for a limited time. A patent gives the inventor the right to prevent others from making, using, or selling the invention.

Hewlett owned the patent but hadn't been able to interest a building-supply company in making the block. Now he thought Fuller might be interested. Why not form a company to manufacture and sell the blocks? It looked like a good business opportunity. After all, Fuller had always worked for other people. Why not try working for himself?

The more Fuller learned about the idea, the more he liked it. Hewlett explained how the blocks could be used in a new kind of system for building walls. First the blocks were put together to form a wall in the usual fashion. They could even be stacked up with nothing between them to hold them together. Each block had two four-inch vertical holes in it, one on each end. When the blocks were interlocked in a wall pattern, the holes were right on top of each other. Concrete poured into the holes formed columns that held the wall together. In this way, a strong wall could be quickly built out of blocks that weighed only two pounds each.

Fuller rolled up his sleeves and got started. He turned a red barn near Rock Hall into a workshop. Like a young Thomas Edison, he started experimenting with different materials. Straw, which Hewlett had used, might not be the best fiber for the purpose. Bucky experimented with this and that. Finally he decided on shredded wood. He also tested different types of cement. He tried adding chemicals that might add strength. At last he found the mixture that would make the strongest block at the least cost.

Now Bucky had to design the machines that would make the blocks. When he was satisfied, he patented his diagrams. Meanwhile, he had to form a legal corporation. Shares of stock were sold to get start-up money. Hewlett, who believed in his son-in-law as much as in his blocks, bought many of these shares. Others were sold to relatives and friends. Fuller was named president of the company, the Stockade Building System.

The factory to make the blocks would have to be

centrally located and near good transportation. After a search, Fuller decided on a place in New Jersey. Getting the blocks into production presented hundreds of problems. Fuller kept going on energy and alcohol. Alexandra's death still weighed on his mind when he had time to think about it. He could still crack jokes and seem happy, but there were signs that things were not well.

One night, for instance, Bucky and Anne gave a party at the Hewlett house. Anne, in a carefree mood, began to flirt with one of the guests. This irritated Bucky. He walked out, apparently to get some air and clear his mind. But he kept on walking. He walked to New York, twenty miles away. Anne didn't hear from him for two days. Then he simply reappeared, explaining nothing. Anne calmly accepted the situation. Life had to go on.

The pressures on Fuller kept mounting. He really believed in the Stockade Building System. The idea made sense. Now he had to prove that it could also make money. This was not easy. The building industry, he found, did not welcome new ideas. Architects designed houses and named the materials that went into them. To play it safe, they used only materials that had been around for years. The building unions, too, fought against anything new. Why should a bricklayers' union accept a better technique if it meant less work for its members? Even when Fuller could get an architect to order and a union to use his blocks, he still had troubles. State and local building regulations—called *codes*—did not mention Stockade blocks. Building and fire inspectors sometimes just said no. Fuller's blocks were not in the code book. And when they said yes, it was often yes…if. Fuller would have to construct a test wall. These walls always passed the tests, but they took a lot of Fuller's time.

In spite of the problems, the Stockade Building System managed to grow. A second small factory was built, and then a third. Bucky was on the road most of the time, away from Anne. When another factory was started near Chicago, Bucky felt he had to be on the scene. He moved to Chicago. Because of her family responsibilities, Anne remained in Lawrence.

That time in Bucky's life was not a happy one. He could see Anne only on trips to the East. On the job, twelve-hour days were common. After work, he visited clubs where liquor was illegally sold. These places were far from wholesome, their patrons worse. Fuller got to know Al Capone and other Chicago gangsters. The whole Stockade experience was remembered later as a blurry bad dream: "During these years I worked terribly hard, but the minute I was through work for the day—I guess I was in a whole lot of pain about our child having died—I would go off and drink all night long and then I'd go to work again. I had enough health somehow to carry on."

By 1926, however, Anne found that her duties in Lawrence had lessened. She joined Bucky in Chicago. They had enough money to rent a nice apartment overlooking Lake Michigan. Bucky did his best to mend his ways. Why not? He and Anne were together again, and the company continued to grow. Stockade had built over two hundred buildings. Five factories were now turning out the blocks for many more. The worst seemed to be over, and the future looked good. It looked even better when Anne told Bucky that she was pregnant again.

Then without warning—as it had so many times in Fuller's life—the tide turned. Hewlett found himself in need of cash. To raise money, he had to sell his shares in Stockade.

Soon after, the shares were bought by the Celotex Corporation. Celotex was a large and powerful building-materials company. Celotex now controlled Stockade. What would this mean to Fuller?

He suddenly found out. The people at Celotex liked the Stockade product. But they didn't like the Stockade management. They thought the company wasn't making enough money. That was the problem. The answer? To fire the company's president, Bucky Fuller.

So once again, Fuller went into free fall. After years of hard work, he was simply pushed out of the business world. Celotex had given him no warning. He received no severance pay, or money given to dismissed workers. Now he had no job, and his record would be labeled a failure.

But, Fuller wondered, was he really a failure? That depended on who was doing the labeling. He tried to see the BIG PICTURE. It was true that the Stockade stockholders were still waiting for fat dividend checks. Fuller had never spelled $UCCE$$ with dollar signs. What money he had made had been put back into the company, to keep it growing. Slowly he had come to realize that others in the building industry were "trying to make money with building, rather than making good buildings." If judged on moneymaking alone, Fuller was ready to label himself a "complete failure." As he was to say many times later, "You have to decide whether you want to make money or make sense." He couldn't do both.

Such thoughts were comforting, but they didn't pay the rent on the lake-view apartment. Bucky and Anne had saved little money. They were stranded in Chicago with almost no bank account. Bucky didn't know how or where to begin looking for another job. His spirits went down and down. His expenses went up and up. In August 1927, Anne gave birth to another baby girl. They named her Allegra, from the Italian for "joyful" or "happy." Bucky was joyful to see a beautiful child he could call his own, but he was hardly happy about life. Allegra was an added responsibility.

Burdened with worries, Bucky started to take long walks around Chicago. He wandered here and there, a solitary figure, alone in the night with his thoughts. Little by little, these thoughts turned to suicide. Why not, really? What did the future offer? He had made a mess of his life so far. Now, did he want to drag Anne and Allegra down into the mess with him? That didn't seem fair to the two people he loved most in the world. Back in 1920, he had taken out a $50,000 life insurance policy. If he died Anne would get the money. That was enough to live on for years. Besides, the Fuller and Hewlett families would be glad to help out. They always had.

In later years, Fuller was to tell the story of his near-suicide many times. Some of the details differed from telling to telling, but in general the story went like this: Late one night Fuller was out on one of his lonely walks. Worry and self-hatred walked at his side. He found himself on the shore of Lake Michigan. The cold wind brought him no comfort. The water must have looked dark, anonymous, inviting. Once again he thought of ending his life. "I had adequate courage to swim out into the lake until I became exhausted and sank."

That swim never started. As Fuller stood by the water, he found himself thinking. He began to think about thinking. He knew he had a good mind. He asked himself if there was any good reason to believe in a mind greater than the human mind. Yes, he reasoned. The orderly universe itself disclosed something he could call God. Then who really knew better about the value of Bucky Fuller's life—God or Bucky Fuller? God, obviously. For Fuller, there was wisdom in realizing that he himself was part of the universe, put here for a purpose. Should he commit suicide? No. "Apparently addressing myself, I said, 'You do not have the right to eliminate yourself. You belong to the universe.... You and all men are here for the sake of other men.'"

From that point, thought tumbled upon thought. Fuller realized that in deciding not to kill himself, he had relied only on his own experience. Perhaps that word was the key to the future: *experience*. Always, he had relied on the opposite of experience: *tradition*. In the very first grade, he had been told to "shut up and learn." He had tried Harvard because it was the thing to do. He had entered the business world because it was the thing to do. Yet both failures had given him a lot of experience. Why, when he thought about it, he had nothing but experience. He had worked with cotton-mill hands in Canada and bankers who controlled big building projects. He had known Vincent Astor and Al Capone. He had certainly learned more than most thirty-two-year-old men. Now he had to think about what it all meant.

Anne Fuller must have been shaken by the plans that fell from her husband's lips in the next few days. Fuller announced that he had been put here on earth for a purpose. That was to understand the BIG PICTURE and then use his findings to help other human beings. To do this, he needed time to study and think. Earning a living, he said, was part of a tradition he chose to ignore. He knew he was penniless. He knew he had a wife and child. He just felt forced to see what he could do, as one determined person, to better the lot of humanity.

Anne must have had her doubts, but she kept her faith in Bucky. They gave up the lake-shore apartment. Looking for a cheap place to rent, they finally found a run-down place on Belmont Street. It was little more than a room in a poor neighborhood. Fuller didn't care. He lived in his own mind. Why had he always just accepted what others wanted him to think? Words, he decided, had had a lot to do with it. The voice of tradition had spoken in words. He himself had learned to throw words around, even with some wit and purpose. But what was he, a parrot? Had he really thought about the words he used? What did simple words like *good* and *bad* really mean? If he had been born in another time and place, things he now called good might be bad indeed. The more he thought about it, the more certain he became. He informed his wife that he was going to stop speaking. He would talk again only when he was sure that each word came from his own experience.

Of course, Bucky broke this vow with little Allegra. He also spoke some to Anne, but not enough to please her. For nearly two years, Anne became Bucky's voice in dealing with the world. It was she who looked after Allegra and dealt with outsiders. Meanwhile, Fuller sat in libraries or at home, reading and thinking. He read history, science, mathematics—all that it now seemed he must know. Sometimes he just sat and thought for hours at a time. Or he would push Allegra's baby carriage throught the streets, lost in a mental city of his own. To make his thinking clear, he started to write. He wrote hundreds of pages, thousands of pages. He tried to connect bits of knowledge in one field

71

with information from other fields. He discovered that every fact he knew was related to everything else he knew. All knowledge was one. To him, art was science, and science was art. The so-called experts were almost ignorant. They learned more and more about less and less. Specialists could never see the BIG PICTURE. In this way a new occupation was born: *comprehensivist*.

Religious is a word often used in connection with this period in Fuller's life. In one version of the story, he hears voices and feels lifted off his feet. Certainly he was "reborn" in a sense. He surrendered himself to a Higher Intelligence. He took a vow of silence. There was almost a vow of poverty. In a way, Bucky seems to have believed that "the Lord will provide."

The Fullers did not eat well, but they did eat. They managed to pay the rent. Allegra received a healthful start in life. Somehow, money always seemed to come to Bucky and Anne just when they needed it. Two older relatives died, leaving the Fullers small sums in their wills. An old friend heard of Bucky's new life and repaid a forgotten loan. The Hewletts and the Fullers helped out at times. Bucky found that when he took life seriously, life treated him with care. He later said, "There's something of the miraculous in all that."

6

Dymaxion Days

R. Buckminster Fuller's decision by Lake Michigan was the big turning point in his life. Before the decision, he had thought of himself as a failure. Supposedly, being a failure was the rule of life. His uncle had told him about it back in 1913. Human beings were born failures. Every man had to prove his right to success and happiness. But now, Fuller realized that the rule was a false one. He saw the BIG PICTURE. Only human beings could discover the scientific laws that governed the universe. That gave humanity a rather honored place in the universe. In a way, human beings were the tools the universe used to understand itself. Could such creatures be called failures? No, not at all. Human life was a great success. Fuller's only trouble was this: He had just one lifetime to spread his new knowledge to every man and woman on the face of the globe.

Fuller rolled up his mental sleeves and set to work. To

Anne Fuller drew this portrait of Buckminster Fuller in 1928.

get more time in each day, he discovered a new method of sleeping. He had long envied the way dogs and some other animals slept. They simply took short naps when they were tired, and woke up refreshed. Fuller tried this himself. He found that he could get along with a half-hour nap in every six-hour period. This gave him a twenty-two-hour workday. Usually, of course, he got more sleep. But when he was busy with a project, an eight-hour workday could be stretched to twenty-two.

The projects came fast. Fuller turned his attention to what he called his Chronofile. This was a chronological—or time-order—file of every piece of paper that had anything to do with his life. As a boy, Fuller had loved to keep things. He saved letters and copies of their replies. He saved report cards and bills and school papers. He clipped and saved scientific articles that interested him. Over the years, he had started to keep these papers in albums. Now Fuller saw his Chronofile as something more than a hobby. It was to illustrate the entire life of an advanced man who was born back in the dark ages of the nineteenth century.

Fuller had spent five bad years in the building industry. It is not surprising that housing was still very much on his mind. Much of the time he spent writing was devoted to houses—what they were now and what they should be. As Fuller saw it, the whole building field was a disaster. The trouble started right with the person who wanted a house built. That person told the architect what he or she wanted. This, to Fuller, was like a patient telling the doctor what was wrong with him or her. The average person knew absolutely nothing about new building materials and methods. Yet the architect, eager for the customer's dollars, would go along.

75

Then the builder would smile and do what was wanted. As a result, the housing industry was stuck in the ways of the past.

Some of Fuller's 1927 writings still survive. In one essay, he makes fun of the building industry. What would happen, he asks, if a car were to be designed and built like a house. First, the man with the money would have to select a car designer from among thousands of designers. Then that designer would come with pictures of other cars and with parts catalogs. The man might select a sturdy bumper made in Indiana, a Spanish roof, and an English flywheel. Then a builder would have to be chosen from among thousands of builders. Building the car would take a long time, since it was a one-of-a-kind operation. Government inspectors would constantly interfere. When the car was finally finished, it would have cost $50,000. (This is about $500,000 in today's money.) Moreover, it would not run well. Probably it would not run at all.

For Bucky Fuller, the housing industry should be just that: *an industry*. Like cars and planes, houses should be made in factories. The most modern materials should be used. Most of all, architects should take advantage of the principle of tension. Tension, or "pull strength," is the opposite of compression, or "push strength." For thousands of years, builders had relied on compression. A stone was put on a stone, or a beam on a beam. Each pushed down on the one below it—on all others below it. As a result, walls had to be thick and strong. Now, however, metal rods and cables of advanced design permitted the use of tension. Walls could be held up from the top, not supported from below. If a wall had to support nothing above it, it could be made entirely of very thin glass.

In 1928, Fuller began sending off drawings of what he

called a 4D Tower House. The whole structure was supported by a thick metal cylinder, or hollow pole. From this central pole hung ten hexagonal (six-sided) decks. A model might look like this: Imagine a strong aluminum cylinder ten feet high and a foot across. This cylinder, or thick pole, is set upright on the ground. Hanging from and around it are ten decks. These enclosed decks are living areas. Machines to heat and cool the dwelling, as well as the plumbing, are in the central pole. The whole structure has a look of lightness and grace.

Science fiction, perhaps? Since the 4D Tower House was to be built in a factory, it would have to be delivered to its permanent location. To do this, Fuller would have used huge zeppelins, or dirigibles. One of these football-shaped monsters of the air would simply hook onto the house and lift it to its site. Then the dirigible would drop a bomb, to make a hole in the ground. The bottom end of the house would be lowered into the hole. Cables would hold the structure in place as concrete was poured around the foundation part of the house. Fuller claimed that the whole building, ready to live in, could be put in place in a single day.

A more practical idea followed. This was a one-family version of the "House on a Pole." Fuller called it the 4D House. A single deck hung from a central pole. Again, all the pipes, wires, and machinery to keep the house going were inside the pole. The living space featured the latest equipment. Having watched little Allegra as she toddled from this danger to that, Fuller made the rooms absolutely safe for children. The house cleaned itself with very little human effort. Dishes were washed and put away automatically. Air mattresses on the beds could be adjusted to the sleeper's comfort. A special learning center featured television, which

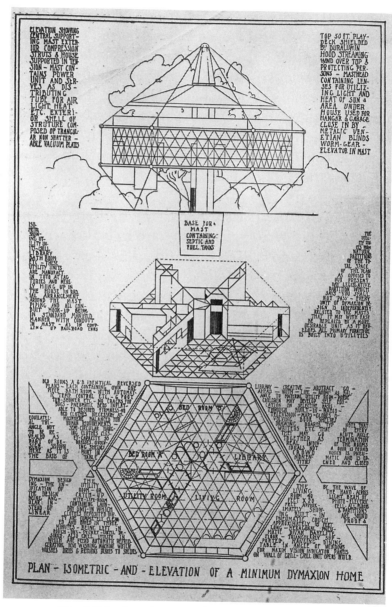

The 1928 plans for Fuller's 4D Dymaxion House.

hadn't even been invented in its present form yet. Nor had the solar power units been invented. Neither had the machine that opened doors with a wave of the hand. Nor had the "fog gun," a skin-cleaning device that used almost no water. Neither had the special toilet that stored waste for later disposal. In fact, the kind of hard aluminum necessary for the house itself was still five years away.

These matters were not serious problems to Fuller. He considered them details. Once the BIG PICTURE of the house was in people's minds, the necessary inventions would follow. The more Fuller worked on his 4D House, the more excited he got. The cost? Fuller investigated the cost per pound of an automobile. Using a slightly higher figure, he announced that his three-ton house would cost $1,500. That low price would be a one-time cost. Because the house required no electric, sewer, or water lines, it could be transported anywhere a family wanted to move. You could live on a Pacific cliff one year and in the Colorado Rockies the next, in the very same house.

Fuller's interest in the 4D House began to draw him out of his own. He began to talk again. He applied for patents. He made a shiny scale model of the house that excited all who saw it.

In 1929, the huge Marshall Field department store in Chicago decided to put on a furniture-of-the-future show. The store thought Fuller and his model house would attract customers. Would Bucky agree? Certainly. The store was by far the largest in Chicago. The show would be just the place for his 4D House. He liked the idea of giving a short lecture several times a day.

Plans for the show went smoothly—except for one thing. The publicity people at Marshall Field wondered about the term "4D House." It didn't sound exciting. What did it mean, anyhow? Fuller explained that the "D" stood for "dimension." The first three dimensions were the usual ones: width, length, and height. The fourth dimension was time, in honor of Albert Einstein. But all Fuller's talk of Einstein and modern science didn't impress the Marshall Field people. They suggested finding a new name, something zingy, with the sound of the future in it. An advertising writer was hired to work with Fuller. He wrote down some words that Fuller often used. Then he separated the syllables and tried putting this with that. By and by he had it: *Dymaxion!*

Dymaxion is a combination of *dy*namic, *max*imum, and *ion*. Fuller liked the new word, too. It became his trademark for many years. And the newly named Dymaxion House was the hit of the show.

Not all of Fuller's efforts were as successful, however. In June 1929, he went to the annual convention of the American Institute of Architects (AIA). It was held in St. Louis, Missouri. Fuller and a friend drove down from Chicago with the model house. Fuller's hope was to do more than just display the house. He really believed that Alexandra would not have died if she had been raised in climate-controlled, dirt-free surroundings. Fuller wanted to give the house to humanity. He offered the patents, free of charge, to the AIA. To his disappointment, the offer was not only rejected, but scorned. Factory-build housing, after all, would have put the architects out of business. Their statement indicated their fears: "Be it resolved that the AIA establish itself on record as inherently [by nature] opposed to any peas-in-a-pod-like reproducible designs."

Fuller made another resolution of his own. He decided that his years of exile in Chicago should come to an end.

Memories of Bear Island acted like a magnet on his mind. Soon Bucky, Anne, and little Allegra were headed back East, back to the salt air and the whispering pines. Bucky wanted to spend the whole summer in the Big House.

The summer of 1929 was a good change for Bucky. He had always been disappointed that Anne really didn't like the rough life. For her, living in the Big House was a little too much like camping. She didn't even like to go sailing. Now Bucky found that Allegra, not quite two years old, seemed just the opposite. Like Bucky, Allegra was stocky and energetic. She loved the waves. She shrieked happily when Bucky took her for short splashes in the icy water. Both father and daughter beamed with pride when Allegra learned to point at a boat and say "sloop," "ketch," or "schooner."

Wanting something to do with his hands, Fuller bought an old cargo boat. The tub was forty-four feet of decay, rust, and trouble. It was wide enough to be called a barge. The low price was a joke. So, nearly, was the purchase. And so, certainly, was Fuller's new name for the antique: the *Lady Anne*. Roger Hewlett, Anne's younger brother, spent much of the summer working with Bucky on the boat named for sister and wife. They cut down tall trees to replace the two masts. They scraped, varnished, and painted. Bucky even managed to talk a local shipyard owner out of a new engine. Roger was amazed at Bucky's ability to swing a fast, shady business deal his way. "He could convince a silkworm that nylon was better," Roger said later. But the engine stayed in the *Lady Anne*, and the boat was to be Bucky's summer toy for another three years.

September came all too soon, and the happy group on Bear Island began to break up. Bucky decided to go to New York City. He thought that New York would be the best place

Buckminster Fuller and the model of his Dymaxion House.

to show the Dymaxion House and to interest people in his other ideas. First he settled Anne and Allegra in a small but comfortable house on Long Island. Then he went off to the big city to preach his message of a better future.

October 1929, however, brought its own kind of message about the future. The sliding stock market made headlines day after day. During the 1920s, the stock market had gone up, up, and up. Not only the wealthy, but also middle-class people had bought more and more shares and had made more and more money. Late in 1929, few people realized that the hot economy of the 1920s had begun to cool down. But when the stock market started down, people grew fearful. They sold their shares, which drove the market down even more. They also tightened their purse strings, which drove the economy down. A recession in 1930 turned into the Great Depression that lasted for years. Many people lost their jobs—and even, as some banks closed, their savings.

As the Great Depression began, Anne and Allegra were safe, living in a nice house in Hewlett, Long Island. Bucky's goal was to keep them there, with the rent paid and food on the table. He tried to join them on weekends. The rest of the time he spent in New York, living on almost nothing. He slept where he could: in a corner of a friend's apartment, in a storeroom atop a warehouse, under the table on which his Dymaxion House was being displayed in a hotel. Sometimes he got along on one meal a day. At one point he took a job he liked—but it ended after a few months. During this difficult period Caroline Fuller helped the family out with a small allowance. But Bucky was too proud to accept much personal help from his mother.

By this time Fuller had built a new model of his Dymaxion House. He could take it apart and carry it around in a large suitcase. In spite of the depression, people still found the house fascinating. Fuller received invitations from as far off as Chicago to give lecture/demonstrations. Some of these invitations were good ones indeed: the Princeton University School of Architecture and the Yale University Architectural School. But Fuller still spent most of his time sitting around New York cafés, talking and drinking coffee. His talk always interested people, and one café owner even paid him in meals to sit at a table and attract customers. Although Fuller liked the café life, what he really wanted was a larger audience.

Late in 1930, Bucky learned that a small architecture magazine calle *T Square* was for sale. A magazine, he thought, would give him the larger audience he needed. Why not buy *T Square* and tell the architects of the country what they really needed to hear? Of course, he would need some money—but once again, Fuller found a way. He cashed in his life insurance policy and bought the magazine.

Bucky Fuller was never a person to do something in the traditional way. This was true with the magazine. First, he changed its name to *Shelter*. Then he canceled all advertising contracts. To accept advertising meant publishing on a regular schedule, which he had no wish to do. Instead, he would publish only when a truly excellent issue had been put together. He raised the price to $2—unheard of! (This would be about $20 an issue today.) Finally, he used his contacts to get articles by exciting, up-and-coming young architects.

Shelter, some experts said, was sure to fail. Young Fuller knew nothing about putting a magazine together and then getting people to buy it. As it happened, however, these experts were wrong. With each issue, *Shelter* sold more and more copies. The magazine was full of new ideas. One issue was devoted to ecology, a subject few people in 1931 had ever thought about. So it came as a surprise when, late in 1932, Fuller decided to close the magazine. He dumped all the articles he had on hand into what he announced was the final issue.

Actually, Fuller's decision was typical of him. He had proved that a magazine like *Shelter* could be a success. That was all he wanted to do. He had no wish to be tied down to a business forever, just because it made money. And besides, he had many other interests to work on. For instance, since his navy days he had been drawing little pictures of a new kind of vehicle. Mainly, it was a small plane with wings that collapsed, powered by what we know today as jet engines. Landing at sea, the vehicle became a fast boat. Coming down onto land, the vehicle turned into a car. Some of these ideas and drawings Fuller had put into the last issue of *Shelter*. Small models of this Dymaxion Vehicle had been displayed with the "House on a Pole."

Fortunately, the article or the model had interested Philip Pearson, a wealthy investor. Early in 1933, Pearson came to Bucky Fuller with a proposal. He would put up the money if Fuller would produce the land-travel version of the Dymaxion Vehicle.

At first Fuller had his doubts. He remembered his years with Stockade Building System. He had worked and worked, only to be forced out because the stockholders wanted more money. Now Fuller told Pearson that he would take the money only if he had *total* control. Pearson was to expect absolutely nothing in return. Even if Fuller decided to spend all the money on ice-cream sodas, Pearson would have nothing to say. That would be that.

Pearson, too, must have had his doubts. But he went on

listening to Bucky's spellbinding ideas. Fuller had figured out that the main problem in future automobile design would be air resistance. Most cars of the time looked something like the most common one, the Model A Ford. They were boxlike, with nearly flat vertical surfaces front and rear. At thirty miles an hour, air resistance was not too much of a problem for a Model A. But Fuller knew that cars of the future might go ninety miles an hour. At ninety, air resistance would be not three times as much as at thirty, but nine times as much. He explained that even going from thirty to sixty, air resistance increased four times. Fuller's streamlined, teardrop design must have been too much for Pearson to resist. He said yes to Fuller's terms. He even went to a safe-deposit box and got the money in cash.

The month of March 1933 was the most depressed point in the Great Depression. Franklin D. Roosevelt, the newly elected president, closed the banks because so many were failing. Businesses everywhere were going belly-up. A quarter of the American work force was unemployed, and those lucky enough to have jobs often found their wages cut. Yet it was in March 1933 that R. Buckminster Fuller found himself in a position to start a new company, the Dymaxion Corporation. In a sad but useful way, the depression was an advantage. Many factories were idle, for sale or for rent. Looking for a place to build the Dymaxion Vehicle, Fuller decided on a small factory in Bridgeport, Connecticut. It had once manufactured the Locomobile; that car company had disappeared with the coming of bad times. Fuller also found that a small employment ad in the paper produced a long line of skilled workers, desperate for the paychecks that would feed their families. Although he needed only twenty-eight people, more than a thousand applied.

Fuller was also able to hire the chief engineer he

wanted, W. Starling Burgess. It was Burgess who had returned to Milton Academy with the thrilling tales of an aviation pioneer. Since that time, Burgess had designed many well-known boats and airplanes. Two of his boats had won the America's Cup. At the time, his name was better known than Fuller's. But Bucky didn't mind. Burgess's math was also better, and that was what mattered.

With Pearson's cash, Burgess's know-how, the workers' skills, and Fuller's energy, the Dymaxion Vehicle rapidly took shape. The motor and drivetrain were modifications of standard equipment. Everthing else—the frame, the body, and many parts—had to be designed and manufactured from scratch. Fuller and Burgess agreed that every piece of the vehicle had to be perfect. There was no such thing as "second best." They also tried to avoid publicity until the vehicle could be rolled out of the factory. It was put together in a back room without windows. Only special people could enter.

After three months of good progress, Fuller ran into real trouble. Without saying anything, the workers were staging a slowdown. Fuller realized their problem. Although the men had been told to expect six months' work at the most, they wanted their jobs to go on. When the Dymaxion Vehicle was finished, their work would be finished also. What could Fuller do? Lecture and threaten the workers day after day? No, he decided. He liked the men too much to turn against them. One day he announced that a second car was to go into production. Of course, he had no idea where the money would come from. But the announcement served its purpose. The first Dymaxion Vehicle was finished on time: July 12, 1933. It was Bucky's thirty-eighth birthday.

A crowd of thousands gasped and marveled as the Dymaxion Vehicle came out of the plant. Used to seeing Model A Fords and 1930 Studebakers, they now saw a teardrop on wheels. Three wheels, to be exact. A pair in the front provided front-wheel drive. A single wheel at the back served to steer the vehicle. The motor was also in the rear, behind a nine-passenger compartment. Fuller tried the vehicle on a small test track near the factory. It handled perfectly. Even with only three wheels, it was more stable than the ordinary car. It could round curves at a faster speed. This was due to three things: the front-wheel drive, the low center of gravity, and the rear-wheel steering.

Almost overnight, the names *Fuller* and *Dymaxion* were in papers across the country. The car was a news photographer's dream come true. Fuller was soon driving from place to place, showing what the car could do and answering questions. He would point out that the car cooperated with nature; it didn't try to fight natural laws. Did a fish guide itself from the front or the back? And who ever heard of a bird that slowed forward progress by steering itself from the front? Bucky loved demonstrating how the vehicle could be parked in a space only a few inches longer than its own nineteen feet. He would nose the vehicle into the curb, nearly touching the car ahead of it. Then he would cut the rear wheel all the way, so that it pointed at the curb. A touch on the accelerator, and the rear of the vehicle slid into the space sideways.

Many people got the see the vehicle, but only a fortunate few were chosen to ride in it. Fuller took the vehicle to New York by special request. This time the fortunate few were a group of top magazine editors. Talking as he drove,

Fuller's Dymaxion Vehicle. The rear wheel steered the streamlined, tear-shaped vehicle, acting much like the rudder of a ship.

Fuller started down Fifth Avenue. Of course, everyone on the sidewalk stopped and stared as the vehicle passed. In those years, a policeman directed traffic at each busy midtown crossing. One policeman held up a stop sign of a hand, and Fuller obeyed. He slowly pulled one front wheel within inches of the officer's foot. Then he cut the back wheel and did a complete circle around the policeman, so carefully that the wheel next to the amazed officer turned in a circle only a foot or so wide. Seeing this, the policeman at the next corner also stopped Fuller. He expected the same demonstration, and he got it. There was a policeman at every corner. It took Fuller an hour to make the planned one-mile trip.

Another of the fortunate few was Amelia Earhart, the famous aviator. She, too, was interested in advanced design. She also understood Bucky's reason for using the term *vehicle*, not *car*. The vehicle was, over time, to become a plane, with collapsing wings and jet engines that hadn't yet been invented. Bucky Fuller and Amelia Earhart became good friends. She told Bucky that she planned to go to Washington, D.C., to accept an award. Eleanor Roosevelt, President Franklin D. Roosevelt's wife, had invited her to stay at the White House. Why couldn't Bucky drive her up to the White House in style—in the Dymaxion Vehicle? Bucky agreed. A photo of Mrs. Roosevelt and the vehicle would get in a lot of papers.

The trip to Washington took longer than planned. Fuller was stopped more than fifty times by curious policemen. But he got the pictures he wanted—and the publicity. Later, Fuller took the vehicle to Chicago, where it was the hit of the 1933 World's Fair. He found that he could get thirty miles on a gallon of gas, sometimes forty. The vehicle's top speed was 120 miles an hour. This amazed even Fuller, for the engine was only ninety-five horsepower. He knew about other cars that could do 120. They had 300-horsepower engines.

In fact, the vehicle had only two disadvantages. Because of its planelike design, it tended to handle a little like a plane when hit by strong winds. Its tail became light. This defect, Fuller felt, could be corrected in later models. Still, to play it safe, only Fuller or someone approved by him ever drove the vehicle. The second disadvantage was an odd, indirect one. Other drivers on the road, like everyone who saw the vehicle, were fascinated. They sometimes forgot their own driving as they stared at the Dymaxion Vehicle. Their eyes left the road ahead. Obviously, this was dangerous—for Fuller as well. Other interested drivers tried to follow the vehicle. Or they would draw up alongside, for a long second look. Some tried to pass, even to race. It was this second danger that led to tragedy.

To get money to finish Dymaxion 2, Bucky was forced to sell Dymaxion 1. It went to Gulf Oil. The company planned to use it in advertising. Al Williams, a Gulf executive, was put in charge of the vehicle. He drove it here and there, with great success. Soon, however, Fuller learned that an English company was interested in the vehicle. The company might buy Dymaxion 2. They might even buy rights to make the car in England. Now the English company was sending an expert to Chicago. Fuller asked Williams to get the Dymaxion 1 to Chicago at once. In turn, Williams hired a professional race driver to take the car from Detroit to Chicago. The driver, a man named Turner, was to demonstrate the vehicle. He was to show the English guest every courtesy.

Bucky was busy in the Bridgeport factory when the news from Chicago arrived. He learned of it from the headlines:

DYMAXION CAR KILLS DRIVER

THREE-WHEELED CAR KILLS DRIVER

FREAK CAR ROLLS OVER, KILLS RACE DRIVER

Fuller rushed to Chicago. On the way, he read every newspaper he could. The stories said that the vehicle had struck some kind of "wave" in the road. It had skidded, then turned over several times.

In Chicago, Fuller slowly learned the whole story. A car driven by a local Chicago politician had started to play games with the Dymaxion Vehicle. The car had followed, drawn up alongside, and tried to race. Turner, annoyed, had tried to outrun the politician. In the race, the politician's car hit the rear of the Dymaxion Vehicle. Both vehicles went out of control. The politician was not seriously injured. But he had influence. His car was towed away before newspaper reporters got to the scene. As a result, the news stories were incomplete. The fact that a park commissioner's car had caused the collision was never mentioned.

The future of the Dymaxion Vehicle crashed with that accident. The true story didn't come out for weeks, and then got only back space in the papers. In the public mind, the vehicle was a killer. Fuller did all he could to correct things. His mother died in 1934, leaving him a little money in stocks and bonds. This he put into still a third Dymaxion Vehicle. With it, Fuller broke the Detroit-to-Chicago speed record. The Chicago World's Fair continued into the summer of

1934, and Fuller demonstrated the vehicle's stability to thousands of people. The crowds said "Oh!" and "Ah!" at Fuller's racetrack turns—but this was, after all, the same kind of car that had killed a man.

Fuller tried other stunts, but nothing seemed to help. In 1934, the few car companies left in business were struggling. Sales were still low. No company had the money to completely retool for a new kind of car. Sadly, Bucky had to close the Bridgeport factory. His mother's stocks and bonds weren't enough to pay off all his debts. He had to sell something else his mother had left him. This was his share of Bear Island.

7

Through War and Peace

In the last fifty years of his life, R. Buckminster Fuller gave hundreds of lectures, maybe thousands. Each lecture contained something new. But through them all, Bucky kept pounding away at a few basic ideas. One of his ideas was this: An action produces both direct *and indirect* results. The indirect results, in the long run, can be more important.

For instance, Fuller would say, consider this example: the honey bee. A bee lights on a flower for a single purpose, to gather a sweet substance called nectar. Yet the bee's action has an important indirect result. On its body, the bee carries pollen from flower to flower. The bee's action results in the cross-fertilization of flowers. Thus more and better flowers grow. Thus more and better bees survive.

WHAT DO YOU THINK YOU'RE DOING?—that's an old question. In Fuller's terms, the question should be this: WHAT *ELSE* DO YOU THINK YOU'RE DOING?

Your actions might produce your own selfish result: Result A. What about the other results? Results B, C, D, and E? Fuller thought that the selfish interests of each human being often stopped progress for all human beings.

Fuller's work on the Dymaxion Vehicle led to an interesting indirect result. Philip Pearson, who had offered the money for the first vehicle, offered the Fullers something more. Pearson and his wife had a summer home not far from the Bridgeport factory. Located in Darien, Connecticut, the Pearson house overlooked Long Island Sound. The Pearsons had been thinking of building a separate dwelling on top of their low garage. Why not let Bucky and Anne design the new house? The Pearsons would pay the bills. The Fullers could live in the house as long as they wanted to.

The Fullers agreed. Bucky, of course, was busy at the Bridgeport factory. Anne took over the design of the new house. She had always been a gifted artist. Now she proved herself equal to Bucky as a designer. Her house plan resulted in a convenient three-bedroom home. Allegra, of course, had her own room. Bucky and Anne shared a double bedroom, and the third was for guests. The house had a living room that led to a porch overlooking the water. Bucky could sit there, after work, watching white sails crisscross the blue bay.

Allegra, by this time, was no longer a toddler. She was a kindergarten kid. Then a first-grader. Fuller watched her progress in the local school.... Progress? Her father doubted it. Fuller had his own ideas about education. He remembered his own years in school: "who beheaded who and who put someone in a tower." Fuller now had his own definition of history: who controlled the resources of the world and who had the power to distribute them. Fuller also felt that all

97

children are born full of curiosity. Throughout their growing years, they want to reach out. First they reach out to touch something, then to learn something. According to Fuller, schools of the time killed this desire in the average child. For the most part, school provided only "a general baby-sitting function." Schools lined kids up in rows and taught everyone the lesson of the day. But why should anyone really care about the lesson of the day? "There is no reason why everyone should be interested in the geography of Venezuela on the same day and hour unless there is some 'news' event there, such as a revolution."

Bucky and Anne looked around for a school that would consider Allegra's interests when setting the lesson of the day. The Dalton School in New York City was the final choice. In the fall of 1934, the Fullers moved to an apartment on East Eighty-Seventh Street, just around the corner from Dalton. Allegra could walk to school without even having to cross a street.

Back in busy New York, Fuller took on new life. Wherever he went, he carried his own excitement with him. The Dymaxion Vehicle had made him somewhat famous. He had always been able to make friends easily. Now he found himself clinking glasses with New York's most brilliant people. (Prohibition had ended in 1933. Liquor was once again legal.) He was invited to join the Three Hours for Lunch Club, a rather select group. Its members included well-known writers like Chistopher Morley and Don Marquis. Cocktails were served, and served again. The table rang with laughter and wit.

Fuller soon became known for his spellbinding talk. Ideas sprang from his mind like popcorn from a popper. The theories of Albert Einstein? Easy, Fuller would say. It didn't matter that his explanation was not exactly easy. People loved his talk all the same. Fuller had a lifelong urge to communicate what he knew to other people. Now, in 1935, his best friends seemed to be writers. He still wanted to reach a greater audience. The result? Fuller decided to write a book himself. Into it he would pour idea after idea. The sleeping world would take notice at last.

Bucky Fuller worked on *Nine Chains to the Moon* well into 1936. The title alone, he thought, would spark interest. What did it mean? Fuller figured that if all the people on earth stood on each other's shoulders, they would form a human chain nine times the distance to the moon. In this way, he wanted to show that the moon wasn't so far away. It was quite within human understanding. So were other places in the universe. So were other far-out ideas.

Nine Chains is an exciting book. Reading it today is rather like trying to keep up with the speed of light squared. Fuller jumps from housing to history to psychology to a dozen other fields. To make important points, he SHOUTS in CAPITAL LETTERS. He predicts that power will be beamed from place to place, like radio waves. He sees huge growth for the western coast of Canada, much more than for the United States. In ten years, he states, mass-produced housing will really take off. A new invention called television will mean a new kind of education. The schoolhouse will disappear. Television will also "smash dictatorships as the hand of man smashes a mosquito." Russia will become an industrial democracy. Another prediction—and a correct one—is that new inventions will make it increasingly possible to *do more with less*. (Fuller would continue to explain this idea throughout his life. The large radio tube of 1936, for instance, has now given way to the tiny transistor.)

When Fuller finished *Nine Chains,* he sent it off to a publisher. The publisher was interested—but worried as well. Fuller had written three chapters on Einstein. He had tried to explain the practical meaning of Einstein's famous equation, $E = mc^2$. At the time, it was commonly said that only a dozen scientists in the world could understand Einstein. Fuller was not known as one of these few geniuses. How could the publisher risk putting Einstein-à-la-Fuller before the public?

Fuller's response was Bucky at his best. At the time, Dr. Einstein was at Princeton University in New Jersey. Why not send the manuscript to Einstein? Then the publisher could see what the great man thought of it. This the publisher did. The next year, Fuller received a call from a Dr. Morris Fishbein. Fishbein said he was a friend of Einstein's. He also said that Einstein wanted to meet Fuller. Would tonight be too soon? At the Fishbein apartment on New York City's Riverside Drive?

That evening R. Buckminster Fuller entered a large, high-ceilinged living room that overlooked the Hudson River. There were quite a few people there, but Einstein singled Fuller out at once. Could they talk privately? They went into a smaller room, a study. Fuller saw the *Nine Chains* manuscript on a table. Einstein sat down on one side of the table, Fuller on the other. Fuller felt himself in the presence of greatness. "Young man, you amaze me," Einstein began. He had not only read the book, but approved of it highly. For years, he had supposed that his work had meaning only for scientists. Now Fuller had shown him that it had a practical meaning as well. Yes, he would be glad to write the publisher a go-ahead letter.

Nine Chains was finally published in 1938. It received some good reviews, but the sales were far from good. The economy was again sliding downhill. People's practical concerns just did not include Einstein. It would be many years before Fuller would try writing another book.

Meanwhile, Fuller had found a job. It was the first permanent position he had taken since the Stockade years. A friend had asked him to be director of research at the Phelps Dodge Corporation. Phelps Dodge was a large copper producer. The company wanted to start manufacturing more metal products. Fuller quickly learned about new kinds of alloys, which are mixtures of different metals. He designed a new kind of brake drum. Then he turned some old plans of his into what he called the Dymaxion Bathroom. A tub, toilet, and sink formed a single unit, to be sold together as a roomlike package. The unit was easily bolted together from four separate pieces. All plumbing was included, so that it needed only single connections for water and drainage. The whole bathroom was only five-by-five feet. It weighed less than the standard tub. Fuller's idea was that a family could move it from house to house, like a stove or a refrigerator.

Twelve Dymaxion Bathrooms were constructed before Phelps Dodge decided to flush the whole project down the drain. For one thing, the company feared trouble from plumbers' unions. (Why should plumbers be willing to install one unit instead of three separate pieces?) For another, a large customer of Phelps Dodge's manufactured such items as toilets and sinks. In business, you just did not displease your best customers. The Dymaxion Bathroom was probably another good Fuller idea. But at the time, Phelps Dodge's business was better off without it.

For Fuller, the Dymaxion Bathroom was far from a failure. Like the Dymaxion Vehicle, it was another product ahead of its time. He was still satisfied with his idea, and his good salary at Phelps Dodge continued. The paychecks more than covered Allegra's school, the apartment, and necessary expenses. There was some money left over for fun. There were good times at Martin's Lane, and better times on Bear Island. (His relatives still owned their shares of the island property.) In New York, Fuller's active social life went on. Talking—and drinkng—his way around the city, he met more and more important people. One of these people was Ralph Davenport, the editor of *Fortune* magazine. In 1938, Davenport offered Fuller $15,000 a year to join the *Fortune* staff. That was a huge temptation (equal to about $125,000 today). Fuller couldn't resist the money.

Or the job. At *Fortune*, Fuller actually wrote very little. His main duty was to spark others with new ideas. *Fortune* was—and is—a business magazine. Part of Fuller's job was to study past business trends in an effort to predict the future. To do this, he took on a huge research assignment. He surveyed the entire progress of discovery and invention, from the beginning of history to 1938. This information he recorded on a number of large charts. The charts were color coded. Discoveries of important ideas and scientific principles were noted in purple. Inventions of a more practical kind appeared in red. Thus the work of a man like Albert Einstein was in purple. The work of a man like Thomas Alva Edison was in red. (Edison, by the way, worked only on inventions he thought would make money. In this way he was Fuller's exact opposite.) When Fuller lectured with his many charts, they completely covered the walls in even a large room. The color coding made an important point clear. "Looking at the charts," he said, " you could see that the purple of the mind was well over the red of matter.

Every time an advance in technology was made it could be traced back to the thinking that had gone on well before it."

This was another idea that Fuller stressed to the end of his days: *mind over matter.* In other words, the invisible over the visible. What are the more important things in life? Fuller would say things that are invisible: love, for instance, or a more complete understanding of nature's laws. The mind and its ideas come first. Edison's phonograph is important only because of the invisible music that comes out of it.

Allegra, however, was concerned with the visible side of Buckminster Fuller. In school she had started the study of dance (which would eventually turn into a career). She had learned how body movements can communicate emotions and thoughts. She also knew that her father was going around giving lectures like a stand-up corpse. When talking, Fuller tended to hold his body stiff as he thought about his words. Now Allegra suggested that he loosen up, more than a little. Bucky wanted very much to do more lecturing. He took Allegra's advice to heart. The expression on his face began to match his vocal expression. He learned to talk with his fingertips, his hands, his elbows—finally his whole body. His listeners saw almost constant motion, a lively mind in action. He demonstrated his ideas with imaginary props. Allegra's suggestion resulted in a speaking style that was to bring her father fame.

Fuller's years at *Fortune* resulted in one more interesting idea: The "energy slave." During most of human history, people had relied on human muscle power for nearly all of their energy needs. Throughout history, too, slavery had been a common practice at different times and places. If someone owned a slave, just how much energy did that slave produce? One way of measuring energy is called the foot-pound. This is the energy it takes to lift one pound a distance of one foot. Fuller figured that a healthy human being, working all day, could produce about 15,000 foot-pounds of energy. Nowadays, of course, slaves no longer do the work. Engines and electric generators provide the power. Engines and generators are the "energy slaves" of the modern age. Fuller got facts on the populations of different parts of the world and the energy produced there. He figured that each person in North America had 347 energy slaves to do the work. In Europe, each person had 27. Africans had 13, and Asians only 2. Thus were the resouces of the world divided.

Fuller was to stay at *Fortune* only about two years. In the summer of 1940, he took a vacation with his writer friend Christopher Morley. Traveling through the rolling farmland of Missouri, Fuller kept seeing huge round grain bins. The bins were made of shining steel. Suddenly an idea hit him: Why not turn a steel grain bin into a house? Excitedly, he explained his thoughts to Morley. A round house provided the most amount of space for the least amount of material. The circular shape was a rigid form. Windows and doors could easily be cut in the bins. Insulation could be added. He could design a kind of Dymaxion roof. If more space was needed, two of the structures could be placed side by side. At the time, millions of Amerian familes were living in shabby houses, even shacks. Here was an answer to the problem—an answer that would probably cost no more than $1,000!

Soon Fuller was in the offices of the company that made the grain bins, Butler Manufacturing of Kansas City. Shortly after that, what he called the Dymaxion Deployment Unit (DDU) was offered for sale. Most of the orders to buy came

This 1941 four-room Dymaxion Deployment Unit was developed to provide cheap housing for defense workers.

from a single source: the government. World War II had already started in Europe. In 1939, German soldiers had marched into Poland. In 1940, as Bucky was working on his DDU, France was falling to the Nazis. The United States, while trying to keep out of the war, was preparing for the worst. The U.S. Army and Navy had an instant need for housing overseas. Other DDUs were needed for civilians working to transfer war materials to friendly nations. Before long, hundreds of DDUs sprouted like mushrooms the world around, from the sands of the North Africa to lonely islands in the Pacific.

If the government made the DDU a success, it was also the government that ended its production. On December 7, 1941, Japanese planes attacked Pearl Harbor in Hawaii. Right away, the United States declared war on Japan, Germany, and the other Axis powers. America's factories turned to war production. Steel was in short supply. Military housing, after all, could be built of wood. But wood could not be turned into guns, trucks, planes, tanks, or ships. Butler Manufacturing could no longer produce the DDUs. Steel was needed for other uses.

Fuller had begun his World War I service sailing the little *Wego* up and down the coast of Maine. Now he decided on something more in keeping with his graying hair. During most of World War II, he sailed into a Washington office every morning and left at closing time. He joined the Board of Economic Warfare early in 1942. Anne stayed behind in New York until Allegra's school year was over. Then the family lived together in crowded Washington. When fall came, Allegra made the daily trip to the exclusive Madeira School in the suburbs.

At this time, also, Fuller made another important decision. He quit drinking. "The war was something serious," he said later. Since 1933, he had done an increasing amount of social drinking. Now, he felt, the war required that he treat himself with sober respect. Also, drinking had begun to affect his life's work, spreading what he called the "design revolution." He found that people didn't listen too closely to a man with a glass of whiskey in his hand. "They think you are just babbling," he said later. "I realized that you cannot drink and be taken seriously as a prophet of the future. So I stopped."

Fuller had vowed to stop drinking before—but he had

never stopped for long. This time he kept his promise. As an added piece of good sense, he stopped smoking as well.

The Board of Economic Warfare couldn't use all of Fuller's amazing energy during the war years. Evenings and weekends, he was free to work on his own projects. One of these projects had been bouncing around in his brain for years: a better map of the world. The maps then in use were, for the most part, those of his own schoolroom days. To show the globe as a flat surface, the maps made some parts of the world look bigger and farther apart than they actually were. This distortion increased as the distance from the equator increased. Thus Greenland appeared to be about the size of South America, instead of only one-sixth as large. Maps using the old-fashioned Mercator projection could not show Antarctica at all.

Fuller zeroed in on a new subject of study: the geometry of the sphere. His system of dividing the surface of a sphere into a number of regular triangles and squares was not a new one; it had been around since the ancient Greeks. But Fuller was the first person to see its possibilities for map projection. He interested the editors of *Life* magazine in the idea. In March 1943, *Life* published what Bucky called—of course!— the Dymaxion Map. Sales of the issue set a record: 3,000,000. People could cut out the squares and triangles of the map, then arrange them in different ways on a flat surface. You could see the world from the point of view of the North Pole, of Antarctica...of wherever. Little tabs on the sections allowed them to be glued together into a kind of globe. Right in the middle of World War II, Bucky's map let people view their world in a new and more accurate way.

In 1944, Fuller left the Board of Economic Warfare. His talents were demanded elsewhere. By that time, Americans began to see that the end of the war was coming at last. Many people started to worry about their jobs. It became almost impossible to keep workers in aircraft plants. What would happen when peace came again? It was feared that the military would have no need for bombers and fighters. The aircraft production lines would grind to a halt. The workers would lose their jobs. For this reason, many people were leaving aircraft factories for jobs that promised more of a future.

Wichita, Kansas, had become an aircraft production center. Several airplane companies had factories in Wichita, among them Beech Aircraft. In 1944, warplanes were still desperately needed. Beech's main problem was to keep workers on the job. How could this be done? One idea was to show the workers that the factory would keep going after the war ended. But if warplanes were no longer needed, what would the factory make?

Houses, of course! Making the body of a B-29 bomber was not really so different from making a metal house. After the war, there would be huge demand for housing. The young men would be coming home, getting married, raising families. And there was that fellow Fuller with his Dymaxion House. He had been preaching the idea since 1928. If two and two ever went together...

Bucky talked to the people at Beech Aircraft. He talked to labor leaders. He talked to the Army Air Force. Soon he had moved to Wichita. He redesigned the Dymaxion House, this time leaving out all that had not yet been invented. Beech gave him engineers and a production crew. Before long, news photographers were recording the construction of the first "House on a Pole."

Fortune gave the Dymaxion Dwelling Machine a gorgeous spread. Pictures appeared in papers from coast to coast. News stories said the house was to cost $6,500. Although the house was not yet offered for sale, over 36,000 orders were sent to Fuller Houses, Inc. Some of these orders contained checks for the full amount. Stock in the new company soared to twenty dollars a share.

But Fuller had been burned in business before. He didn't want to move too fast. The house would not go on sale until all problems were solved. And there *were* problems. He had designed the house so that no piece weighed more than ten pounds. The whole house could be packed into a single crate that a big truck easily could carry. But to put the house together, a special truck with a long boom on the back was needed. In most communities, no such truck could be found. Also, the old problem of building codes would have to be solved. Moreover, the electricians' and plumbers' unions were ready to fight the new house if it cost their members jobs. The Dymaxion Dwelling Machine came with the wiring and plumbing already assembled. Now both national unions said that their members would have to be paid to take all the wiring and plumbing apart, then paid again for reassembly.

Bucky thought he could solve these problems. But he knew it would take time. He jolted his backers when he told them just how much time: seven years. Wow!—that would be 1952! This wasn't what the factory workers wanted to hear. It wasn't what the businessmen involved wanted to hear. *Seven years?* Couldn't Fuller be reasonable? Didn't he realize that he could make half a million on stock deals alone? But Fuller stuck to his forecast. Discussions turned into arguments. The words were raw and very angry.

Fuller had arranged things so that without Fuller, there could be no Fuller Houses, Inc. And quite suddenly, there was no Fuller on the scene. Not many months after the war ended, Fuller's company came to an end also. As with the Dymaxion Vehicle, he simply decided to close up shop. He would move back East, to be with Anne and Allegra.

Because of Allegra's schooling, Anne had never gone to Wichita. Now Allegra's graduation from high school presented Bucky with an odd personal decision. Like her father, Allegra was a whiz at science and math. Bucky had encouraged her to apply to the Massachusetts Institute of Technology (MIT). He wanted her to follow him as a design science pioneer. MIT accepted Allegra. This was something of an honor, for at the time the famous scientific school had only six women enrolled. Bucky felt honored as well—until he talked to Allegra. She said that she wanted to go on studying what she really liked most: dance. Bucky believed in math, engineering, and the coming design science revolution. But he also believed that people learned best what they really wanted to learn. Two of Bucky's strongest opinions came head to head. He solved the problem by sending Allegra into the New York dance world with his blessing. Her needs, he realized, had to overrule his.

Even before Bucky's return from Wichita, Anne had rented a small apartment in Forest Hills, New York. This was not far from Allegra's dance classes in Manhattan. Bucky liked the apartment too. With the Wichita disaster behind him, he decided to take some time off for thought and study. For one thing, he needed to bring his Chronofile up to date.

The period turned out to last for two years. In many ways, it was like 1927 and 1928, the silent time that had followed the Stockade disaster. But now Bucky was far from silent. He kept up with his friends and made new ones. He continued to speak in public, wherever and whenever he could. He had to show people that in spite of Wichita, R. Buckminster Fuller was not a failure.

If *failure* was the word, Fuller had failed only to make money. Yet since 1927, he had put moneymaking behind him. In fact, he despised people who put making money ahead of making sense. In 1947, he told an audience about a new company he was forming. "Obnoxico" was clearly a joke. The company would make only the most obnoxious of products. Yet it was certain to make millions out of the horribly poor taste of some people. The first product, Bucky said, would be this: The last diaper worn by a baby would be stuffed with paper and sent to Obnoxico. The company would plate the diaper with silver or gold. Then it would be returned to the proud parents, "to be filled with ferns and hung in the back window of your car."

Friends sent Bucky other ideas for a promised Obnoxico catalog. Then he announced that he was giving up the project—because it was so sadly sure to be successful. And this may have been true. In later years, Bucky was to comment on the increasing number of "Obnoxico items" for sale everywhere. One example he noted: a toilet seat made of dollar bills embedded in clear plastic. Other examples anyone could find—by the thousands.

8

The Dome Man

As the name suggests *The American Scholar* is a most serious magazine. It is read by people of learning in many fields. On its editorial board are some of the top minds in the sciences and the arts.

Soon after World War II, one of these minds belonged to Harlow Shapley, a famous astronomer. One day Shapley gave the editorial board what he thought was a good idea. Bucky Fuller, he said, should be asked to write an article. "I suppose," Shapley added, "that he's the brightest man alive."

The response was like a sudden roar of snow-chilled wind. Bucky Fuller? The brightest man alive?

"An eccentric!" snorted one board member.

"A crackpot!" shouted another.

Shapley pointed out that such words had once been used for people like Galileo and Einstein. But his arguments got nowhere. The board just did not believe that R. Buckminster Fuller belonged in a scholarly magazine. And in fact, it would be about twenty years before the magazine printed anything by Fuller.

What accounted for this rise in Bucky's reputation? Most of the answer can be put in three words: *the geodesic dome*. By 1966, when *The American Scholar* opened its pages to Fuller, the dome had made him famous. "Oh yes," people would say, "Fuller, the dome man."

Fuller's two years of study, 1947 and 1948, were not entirely without relief. In the summer there was Bear Island, as always. By this time, Fuller had managed to buy back his share of the property. Once again, he could be with his relatives as a rightful owner. The depression days were over. So were the days of the creaking *Lady Anne*. Now Bucky had the money for a sleek yacht. He spent many breezy afternoons teaching Allegra to sail.

Most of 1947 and 1948, however, Fuller spent in the Forest Hills apartment. He brought his Chronofile up to date. Also, he had to learn more about the geometry of the sphere. An idea had been bubbling in his brain since his work on the Dymaxion Map: Why wasn't the dome—a part of a sphere, after all—the lightest, strongest, and most logical structure a person could build? His map work had taught him about great circles. A *great circle* is the largest circle one can draw on the surface of a sphere. (The equator, for instance, is a great circle. So is a circle passing through both of the earth's poles.) Fuller discovered a way to put thirty-one great circles on a sphere so that the entire surface became a network of triangles. Cut such a sphere in half, and you have two domes.

The more Bucky worked at it, the more his mind tingled with possibilities. Of all solid shapes, the sphere encloses the most space with the least amount of surface. Of all flat shapes, the triangle is the most rigid. So a dome made of triangles was both the most economical and the strongest of all building systems. This idea put the old Stockade Building System back into the Stone Age.

In the language of geometry, a *geodesic* is part of a great circle. Fuller's first domes, then, were made of geodesics that ran from edge to edge. Before long the little Forest Hills apartment was crowded with models. Bucky turned to other geometrical ideas. There is a somewhat sphere-shaped form called an *icosahedron*, made of twenty equal triangles. Each of the twenty triangles can be subdivided into nine smaller triangles. When that is done, something of a miracle occurs. Each of the smaller triangles becomes a pie-shaped section of either a *pentagon* (five-sided figure) or a *hexagon* (six-sided figure). Moreover, the pentagons and hexagons overlap, so that each small triangle forms a part of three of the larger figures. (You may be able to observe this pattern by looking at a Fuller dome yourself. Most of the figures will be six sided, or hexagons. A few, where the points of the basic icosahedron touch, will be five sided, or pentagons.)

Now Bucky's tabletop models were strong beyond belief. But to make a really large dome, he knew, would take months of tiresome work with numbers. From a distance, all the short rods that make up a geodesic dome seem to be the same length. In fact, however, they are not. The strength of the whole dome depends on very exact measurements. In those days, of course, Bucky had neither computer nor calculator to help him. He had to figure out these measurements one at a time. He used an old adding machine, and the job took months.

Meanwhile, Bucky gladly left the apartment for lecture

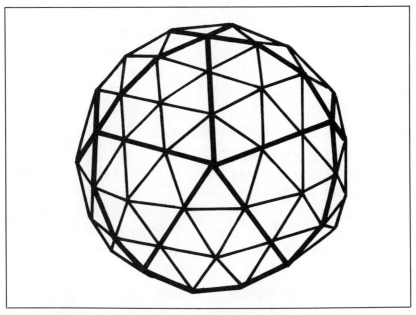

The heavy lines show the pattern of an icosahedron placed over the pattern of triangles on the top three-fourths of a sphere.

dates. In 1947 one of these took him to Black Mountain College, an experimental school in North Carolina. He liked the informal surroundings and the eager students. In 1948 he returned to Black Mountain for the summer session, and again in 1949. Driving to North Carolina, Bucky told Anne that he was now absolutely sure of it: The geodesic dome was the shape of the future. The trouble was that he didn't have the money to experiment on a greater scale. How much money would it take? A lot—about $30,000. It happened that Anne had just inherited some IBM stock. If she sold it, the money would make a real difference to Bucky. Would he accept it? Even as a loan? He certainly would.

Anne's faith in Bucky started to pay off soon after he reached Black Mountain College. Using thin aluminum rods, Bucky and his students put together a fourteen-foot dome. They tested it with their weight. It held up. A picture taken at the time shows nine husky men hanging from little more than a spider's web of structure. The geodesic dome was a success.

Back in Forest Hills, there was now more room in the apartment. Allegra had liked her dance classes, but she found that they led to something more. She wanted not only to dance on the stage, but also to learn about the dance as an art form. How had dance developed in different parts of the world? Just how did body movements communicate? At the time, questions like these could be studied in very few places. One was Bennington College in Vermont. Allegra applied and was accepted, with a scholarship.

Part of Bennington's program gave students off-campus experiences. Allegra's jobs included, finally, working for a motion picture company. Among its members was Robert Snyder, a gifted young director. He and the graceful, dark-haired, deep-blue–eyed Allegra became good friends. Their friendship grew ... to the point where they mentioned marriage to Bucky and Anne. The father probably remembered his own trouble with the older generations back in 1916. He smiled his approval. But the mother was not about to smile. *Motion pictures* meant *Hollywood*, and Hollywood meant ... well, wasn't there another scandal in nearly every paper? Did Allegra really want to get mixed up in *that* crowd?

Yes she did—if that was where love led her. Anne Fuller clamped a lid on her doubts, and even managed a smile. Allegra Fuller and Bob Snyder were married in 1951. Anne grew to like Bob more and more, and finally even she agreed that the marriage was a good one indeed.

By the time of Allegra's marriage, Bucky's domes were taking him places. Literally. He could now charge a thousand dollars for a lecture, and he was on the road more and more. Pulling a trailer full of demonstration materials, he drove from place to place like a salesman of the future. Some of his lectures were one-shot talks before groups of architects or engineers. Other appearances were like mini-courses, at MIT, Cornell, Dartmouth, and other colleges. Fuller would stay on the campus for some time. He would teach students and often use their help to make domes or other structures. Still, however, Bucky was selling the dome mainly as an idea. No big company offered him the big bucks for the big dome that would be the big break.

That break finally came late in 1952. The Ford Motor Company had a problem that its engineers couldn't solve. For years, the center of Ford's activities had been a curious building next to its enormous River Rouge plant in Michigan. The Ford Rotunda was a round structure with an open courtyard. It had originally been built for the Ford exhibit at the 1933–34 World's Fair in Chicago. Then it had been taken apart, piece by piece, and moved to Michigan. As the headquarters building, it was to house the ceremony that would honor Ford's fiftieth year in business. That date would come in April 1953. Festivities were being prepared for the big event. Yet all could be ruined by another event not uncommon in a Michigan spring: rain.

Couldn't the courtyard in the Ford Rotunda be covered? No, said the engineers. Even the lightest roof would weigh 160 tons. Built as a temporary structure, the Rotunda could not possibly support this load. Then Buckminster Fuller was called in. He not only looked at the problem, but solved it quickly. An aluminum geodesic dome, he said, would weigh

A geodesic dome used in industry in Baton Rouge, Louisiana.

only eight and a half tons. The building could easily support it. The cost? Less than the people at Ford had planned to pay.

Fuller signed a contract with Ford in January 1953. He had spent years on the math, so the plan rapidly took shape. Soon the first of about 20,000 aluminum rods went into place. Day by day, the strange new kind of roof grew larger. Some of the Ford engineers looked at the dome with wonder—and at each other with doubt. They shook their heads. Without telling Fuller, they made arrangements with another company. When Bucky's dome collapsed, Ford would be spared the embarrassment. The carcass of the doomed dome would be hauled away with all possible speed.

The Ford engineers need not have worried. In fact, Fuller had overdesigned the dome. It contained a built-in octet truss, another Fuller invention. When the big day arrived, the ceremony went off as planned—except for the "Oh's" and "Ah's" at the ninety-three foot span overhead. The dome was big news.

With the Ford dome behind him, Fuller could almost pick and choose his projects. In 1927, he had predicted that factory-built housing would be delivered by air. Now, in 1954, *The New York Times* carried a front-page photo of a U.S. Marine helicopter lifting a thirty-foot Fuller dome to another site. In 1954 also, Fuller received the first of his honorary degrees. North Carolina State University, in Raleigh, made him a Doctor of Design. The Harvard castoff must have looked at that diploma with particular delight.

...As he certainly regarded another document: his patent on the geodesic dome. No one could build a geodesic dome without Fuller's permission. This permission usually meant 5 percent of the total cost. Fuller's income went up and up, peaking finally at $1 million a year. The U.S. Air Force bought hundreds of radomes (radar domes) for use near the Arctic Circle. Playdomes became common in parks and schoolyards. Orders poured in...for a concert hall...for a railroad repair yard...for a bird enclosure at a zoo. Huge Fuller domes came to stand for the United States at fairs around the world. They were eye-catching, easy to put up, and inexpensive. Bucky himself, often with Anne at his side, traveled to many foreign countries. In Moscow, Soviet Premier Khrushchev gazed up at a 200-foot dome and paid Bucky an odd sort of compliment. All Russian engineers, Khrushchev said, should take lessons from this American master, "Mr. J. Buckingham Fuller."

Fuller spent the money nearly as fast as it came in. Little of it went for himself. Most of the dollars supported his pet projects, all part of the design revolution. Bucky was a president here, a senior partner there, a consultant almost everywhere. Meanwhile, he was hurrying from lecture to lecture, from award to award. He worked on articles and books when others would be sleeping. All this activity could not be run from a little apartment in Forest Hills.

In 1959, Southern Illinois University (SIU) made Fuller an outstanding offer. He would get a good salary, an office, and a staff. He would be named Research Professor. In return, he would have to give SIU a few weeks a year. The rest of the time he would be free to lecture, to do research, and to write. In short, SIU wanted to share the spotlight of Fuller's fame. Bucky very much wanted a headquarters. The two needs went together, and the Fullers soon moved to Carbondale, Illinois. Bucky quickly designed a house—a dome, of course, made of plywood and painted blue and white. Now "the dome man" lived in a dome himself. Anne

Anne and Buckminster Fuller inside their Carbondale, Illinois, home.

liked the house, too, for the most part. "The bad thing was you could not hang paintings because they would be just sort of dangling out from the curve."

Doctor of Design...Research Professor...Famed inventor of the geodesic dome. What more could the future hold for R. Buckminster Fuller? In 1962 he found out. Harvard University wanted to name him the Charles Eliot Norton Professor of Poetry, a one-year position.

Bucky Fuller? A professor of poetry? This offer was confusing at first. How could he accept it? Wasn't he already a professor at SIU? Then he learned that the appointment was mainly an honor. It would require very little time. He wouldn't actually have to move to Cambridge, Massachusetts, where Harvard is. A few lectures would be enough. Also, Harvard used the word *poetry* in a very general way. The honor went to people of vision, whatever their skill with words. So with great pride, Buckminster Fuller returned to the same Harvard that had expelled him nearly fifty years before.

And in fact, Bucky Fuller was something of a poet. Even in his youthful Harvard days, he could come up with funny little poems on the spot. His serious poetry had started later, when he worked at Phelps Dodge. As a writer, Fuller always tended to use big words and long sentences. For this reason, the top people at Phelps Dodge had trouble understanding his prose. One day a fellow worker told him that his writing made much more sense when Fuller read it aloud. Why? Bucky's friend pointed out that when he read, he broke his endless sentences up into short units of thought. Couldn't he break his sentences apart this way on a piece of paper? Fuller tried the idea. Instead of writing margin to margin, he stopped at the end of each thought unit, then went on to a new line. The result looked very much like poetry. When his subject was a serious one, it even sounded very much like poetry. And at its best, it certainly *was* poetry:

And as we gaze around
The starry heavens
We see right now
Live shows of "yesterdays"
Ranging from millions to sextillions of years ago,
As we look at the stars
We see all of history
Now alive.

Later in life, when he wanted to reach an ever-wider audience, Fuller found that his own personal kind of poetry was often the way. Many readers found his books of poetry easier to understand than his prose works.

Fuller's honorary degree from North Carolina State was the first of many. He probably became the most honored man in the United States. The list of his awards runs on for pages. One honor, however, had a very special meaning for Fuller. This honor it was Fuller's privilege to give, not to receive.

The best-known Fuller dome was the one he and the brilliant young architect Shoji Sadao designed for the 1967 World's Fair in Montreal, Quebec, Canada. (With no formal training as an architect, Fuller never had more than an honorary license. For legal and other reasons, he usually worked with a licensed architect.) The dome served as the United States pavilion, or exhibit hall. This Expo '67 dome was 250 feet in diameter. To see it was to catch your breath. Some called it the "skybreak bubble." Others said "Buckminster Cathedral." Its thin plastic skin seemed transparent

Fuller's "skybreak bubble" at the Expo '67 World's Fair in Montreal, Canada.

at times. At other times, the weather conditions made it seem like a floating silver sphere. (Actually, it was three-fourths of a sphere, so that the walls sloped outward as they began to rise.) After dark, under the play of lights, it was a gem of perfection against the night sky.

Soon after the fair opened, Bucky took Anne north to Montreal for a look. Their fiftieth wedding anniversary was approaching, so it was a special trip for both. The United States pavilion stood on an island in the St. Lawrence River. To reach it, people had to pass through a tunnel. For a time Bucky and Anne stood by the tunnel exit, watching people as they stopped to blink at the "skybreak bubble" for the first time. According to Bucky, most people blurted out, "How beautiful!"

Then Fuller had a sudden memory. It went back even more than fifty years. His mother had shown him pictures of the Taj Mahal in India. For more than three hundred years, the Taj Mahal had been considered by many to be the most beautiful building in the world. It had been built by a ruler as a memorial to his beloved wife. Caroline Fuller had explained that the beauty of the Taj Mahal had little to do with the structure itself. No, the building was beautiful because the builder's love had been beautiful. Again, it was mind over matter. The invisible over the visible.

Bucky felt that the "skybreak bubble" was rather like his own Taj Mahal. It would be his golden wedding gift to the person who had loved and supported him for so long. The "Expo Taj," he told Anne, is "pure fallout of my love for you."

CHAPTER

9

Spaceship Earth

"I've often heard people say, 'I wonder what it would be like to be on board a spaceship,' and the answer is very simple. What *does* it *feel* like? That's all we have ever experienced. We are all astronauts."

That's what Buckminster Fuller was telling audiences around the world as the huge Montreal dome rose toward the sky. In a sense, Fuller himself wanted to rise even above the dome—this dome, that dome, any and all domes. Domes were very visible things, after all. They were eye-catchers. But they had little to do with the BIG PICTURE. What Fuller really wanted was a mind-catcher. Perhaps he found it in the term *Spaceship Earth*.

How is the earth like a spaceship? Fuller would go on to explain. As part of the whole universe, our planet is a tiny, tiny object—only about 8,000 miles across. It speeds through space at about 67,000 miles an hour. It also spins around like a top. "Each minute we both spin at one hundred miles and zip in orbit at one thousand miles. That is a whole lot of spin and zip." Light and heat come from a kind of mother ship, the sun. But except for that, the earth *is entirely on its own.* There is no happy landing ahead. Spaceship Earth is in orbit forever. What happens to it is largely up to the human race. When a person buys a car, he or she gets an operating manual with it. But with the earth, there is no operating manual. According to Fuller, we astronauts will have to write that manual as we spin on through space.

And how are we doing? Terribly, thought Fuller. We astronauts on Spaceship Earth spend much more money on weapons than we do on repair of the human race. Nearly half of us are illiterate, hungry, or both. We have organized ourselves into about 150 countries. Hence, 150 admirals are fighting for control of the ship. One side of the ship tries to sink the other. The stern threatens to break off. Meanwhile, fossil fuels—the earth's original oil and coal—are being used up in a no-tomorrow binge. This is like "burning your house-and-home to keep the family warm on [a] cold midwinter night." Atomic weapons threaten to blow the whole place apart. Pollution affects our minds as well as our atmosphere. In fact, the planet may have to be renamed "Poluto."

More than 5 million people attended the World's Fair in Montreal and saw the Fuller dome. Few of these people, however, knew that Fuller originally saw the dome as having an important use. Inside the huge shell, there would be an immense map of the world. There would also be computers programmed with information on the earth's resources. Where were the earth's great stores of water power? How could electricity be transferred from here to there? If the rain forests were destroyed for lumber and food, what would

Fuller lectures about the World Game. Behind him is his Dymaxion Map.

happen to the balance of nature? Did it really make sense to raise beef cattle in crowded Japan? If not, where could the Japanese get their meat? What could the Japanese best offer other people? For years, Bucky had been gathering such information at his SIU headquarters. He know where the world's resources were. He knew distribution patterns. Now it was all on computers, ready to go.

Fuller called it the World Game. (The term *war games* had been used for years by military planners.) Inside the Expo '67 dome, teams of scientists, world leaders, and ordinary people would play the game. The teams would play "against" each other only to solve the world's problems. Everyone would win—because the whole world would win. For instance, take the problem of hunger. The "winning" team would be the one that first solved the problem of providing everyone with food in the most sensible way. Then other teams would go on to other problems: energy, health care, housing, education, and so on. Fuller's aim was to demonstrate that the world's problems could, in fact, be solved. What better way to celebrate the importance of a great "World's Fair"?

Unfortunately, Fuller's World Game idea was not accepted by the United States government. Instead, the dome housed a show called Creative America. Many people yawned at the exhibit.

Fuller was determined to turn this minus into a plus. He stepped up his speaking schedule to over a hundred lectures a year. He took his World Game to Washington, D.C., and then around the world. Airplanes carried him millions of miles. For years he wore three watches. One showed the time back in Carbondale. Another showed the time where he was. The third showed the time at the next stop. Fuller's energy kept him going long after a normal man would have retired. He could still take a half-hour catnap, then wake up ready to take on another piece of the world.

Nevertheless, Fuller did have health problems. As he approached seventy, he felt himself slowing down. The old spin and zip were gone. Part of the trouble, he thought, might be his weight. Years of eating out had helped him put on the pounds. Fuller attacked this problem in his typical fashion: mind over matter. He thought that too much of his body's energy was spent digesting carbohydrates he didn't really need. What his body really needed was protein. The diet he finally decided on was an odd one. He ate lean steak three times a day, lots of it. Along with the steak came something light—applesauce, a salad, fruit, or Jell-O. Some people called the diet dangerous, but Fuller stuck to it. His old energy came surging back. Before long he was down to 140 pounds, an ideal weight for his five feet, six inches, and his stocky build.

Hearing problems also troubled Fuller. Some help came from a hearing aid, but he never entirely solved the problem. Eventually he came to need someone on the stage with him, to field questions from the audience. Also, Fuller developed a noticeable limp. It seemed to be more than the return of his old football injury. Finally it was found that one of his legs was three-quarters of an inch shorter than the other. A steel hip joint later gave some relief. And in his late seventies, Fuller learned that even he could be felled by too much work. On a trip to California he suddenly collapsed. He was rushed to the hospital. Was it a heart attack? No, the doctors discovered. Fuller was simply an exhausted man. After a good rest, he was back on his travels again.

Even during these busy years, however, Fuller always reserved the month of August for Bear Island. There, beyond the reach of even a telephone, he could catch up with his thoughts. He could look up at the stars. The salt air always seemed charged with new life. On Bear Island he could relax—if that was what Bucky Fuller ever did for long. He bought and sailed a series of ever-sleeker yachts. He invented and patented what he called a "Rowing Needle," a twin-hulled boat propelled by oars. Most of all, he enjoyed talking, joking, and laughing with his relatives. His sister Rosy, the informal Bear Island manager for years, finally gave up the job. Leslie Larned, Bucky's niece, took over. Allegra and Bob came from California. Bucky particularly liked the company of his grandson, Jaime Snyder. Bucky had never had a son. Now he watched Jaime grow up with the same tender concern he had once shown for Allegra.

If Fuller had an aching regret as he grew older, it was

probably this: He had never found time to write his great book. For years—in speeches, articles, and smaller books— he had thrown out hints. The great book would explain what he called *synergetic geometry*. This was to be a geometry based on the visible world. (Schoolroom geometry, Fuller thought, had little relationship to what actually existed.) More than that, it would be a geometry of thought. Another claim was that the basic building blocks of nature were not blocks at all but tetrahedra, or four-sided pyramids. Bucky even signed a contract to write the book...but no pages appeared. He was simply too busy.

Then, in 1969, another piece of the famous Fuller luck appeared. It appeared in the form of a man named E. J. Applewhite. As it turned out, Applewhite, in his own way, was almost as interesting a person as Fuller himself.

Ed Applewhite was a tall, scholarly man. A distant relative of Anne's, he had known Fuller, on and off, for years. In 1969 Applewhite decided to retire early from government service (the Central Intelligence Agency). He wanted to devote his talents to something truly important. One day he walked into Fuller's Carbondale office and offered his sevices. What could he do? The two men talked at some length. At last they decided that Applewhite would help Fuller write the big book.

Fuller's staff at Carbondale helped Applewhite gather his materials. Fuller's books, articles, handwritten notes, letters, drawings, unpublished writings, hundreds of hours of lecture tapes—all began to pile up in Applewhite's Washington, D.C., home. Applewhite began typing notes on index cards. It soon became clear that the book would have to go beyond geometry, since the Fuller mind seldom considered one thing at a time. Onto his cards Applewhite copied Fuller's sentences exactly. He went on typing...and typing...and typing. Eventually he would end up with 22,000 cards.

Then the cards had to be put in order. When a series of sentences seemed to fit together, Applewhite would type them out as a manuscript. He typed with triple spaces between lines and left wide margins, so that Fuller could make changes and additions. Fuller did this as he found the time. If Fuller had a few hours between planes, Applewhite could fly to the airport. They often worked in hotel rooms. Carbondale was a poor place for such efforts because of interruptions. More often, Fuller would find a few hours or days to work at Applewhite's home in Washington. Fuller would change and add, change and add. Applewhite would make sure that Fuller's words made sense to others, then go on typing. Some pages went through seven drafts. Fuller's mind connected everything to everything else. He had to keep adding, adding, adding.

Finally, after four years of constant work, Applewhite was finished—or so he tought. The book was now in the hands of the publisher. But when the printed sheets were returned for correction, Bucky seemed far from finished. He couldn't limit himself to a small change here and there. No, he insisted on adding still more. He added so much that the whole book had to be printed for a second time—at Fuller's expense.

Synergetics—all 876 pages of it—finally came out in 1975. Most readers found some pages easy and interesting, other pages nearly impossible. The reviews were good. According to Applewhite, most reviewers probably decided "not to tangle with a text they could not master." They tended to treat the book "as a gorgeous intellectual toy." But

Fuller himself was far from satisfied. He still wanted to add to it. He and Applewhite soon set to work on *Synergetics 2*, published four years later.

Meanwhile, Fuller had changed his headquarters. In 1972 he moved from Carbondale to Philadelphia. Four Pennsylvania colleges had offered him generous support. Fuller became World Fellow in Residence at the University City Science Center. Actually, the move was more of a change for Anne. She loved the culture of Philadelphia and the East. Bucky was still away most of the time, jumping from lecture to lecture.

Even as he neared eighty, Bucky felt that he had to go on speaking. There were at least three reasons for this. First, he could get $5,000 or more for a major lecture. He needed the money for his many projects. These ranged from real possibilities to far-out ideas. A huge floating city nearly became a reality near Baltimore, Maryland. Called Triton City, it was to be a complete community for 5,000 people. Bucky never gave up on the project. Harder to imagine is his fantastic Manhattan Dome. It would have covered midtown Manhattan, from the Hudson to the East River, from Twenty-Second Street up to Sixty-Second Street. A most practical idea, said Fuller. The height of the two-mile dome would make it invisible. The weather would be controlled. Heating and cooling costs for all contained buildings would be next to nothing. And even harder to imagine is Fuller's Cloud Nine, an amazing city in a floating sphere. A sphere half a mile across, Fuller said, would float in air if the inside temperature were just one degree warmer than the outside temperature. It was perfectly possible for people to live in the clouds.

Another reason Bucky kept speaking was that he was so

good at it. He never wrote out a lecture and seldom planned one. Instead, he would start by standing before a crowd with his eyes closed, his hands together in front of him. Slowly he would begin speaking, quite simply at first. Then his mind would find sudden links between this subject and that. He spoke at over 7,000 words an hour. He raced from idea to idea, from example to example. The examples were always good ones. For instance, in the early 1970s Fuller was shocked that the world was spending $200 billion a year on war budgets. Now, just how much money is $200 billion? To most people, big numbers are just big numbers; they all seem alike, beyond the mind's grasp. Fuller would ask people to imagine piling up new dollar bills. Two hundred of them make an inch. Go on stacking up the bills. By and by, the pile gets so high that it falls over. But somehow go on adding bills to the fallen stack...out of the room, out of the building. Suppose someone started in New York. Two hundred billion dollar bills would take that person to San Francisco, across the Pacific Ocean, through Asia and Europe, and back to New York. Around the world!

Fuller seemed to have a special feel for any kind of audience. Years before, little Alexandra had taught him to believe in mental telepathy. Was the crowd bored? Fuller would know. Were they interested? He knew that, too. He could tell by their eyes. Once Fuller was asked to speak to a group of prisoners at San Quentin. He talked for seven straight hours; no one wanted to break the spell. Another time, he addressed a Chicago street gang called the Young Lords. The meeting was held in a cold church basement. People sat shivering, but no one left. Fuller was especially good with children. One evening he sat in the California living room of his friend Hugh Kenner. A cheerful fire blazed on the hearth. Three-year-old Lisa Kenner suddenly broke into the adult conversation. It was a typical *why* question of a typical kid: Why was the fire hot? Bucky took it seriously. "You remember, dear," he began, "when a tree was alive, and gathering in the sunlight?" Here he imitated a tree, his body the trunk, his arms and face the gathering, grateful branches. "Then someone cut the tree down, and sawed it into logs. Some of the logs came here." He pointed at the fireplace. "And what you are seeing is the sunlight, unwinding from the log."

The third reason Fuller kept speaking until he died was the most powerful one. His own honesty wouldn't let him stop. He felt forced to go on spreading his vision of a better world. The way we think about ourselves and society, he said, is based on past possibilities for the human race. In other words, we use yesterday's answers for today's problems. *But the present possibilities for humanity are entirely different.* This difference is a truly revolutionary one. In the past, only a few people could enjoy a high standard of living. Wealth and comfort were in short supply. There wasn't enough food or anything else to go around. Life was a matter of "you *or* me." My kind of people or your kind of people. My country or your country.

But by 1970, Bucky said, he could demonstrate that the good life was possible for all the world's people. Then: "You *or* me." Now: "You *and* me." What will it take to get there? In a word: cooperation. Not weaponry but "livingry" is the key to the future. "War is obsolete." Increasingly, we will do more and more with less and less. The average person will have to "work" only about fourteen years in a lifetime. *Politics, war, weapons,* and *debt* will be words of the past. "Earning a living" will no longer mean "earning the right to

During the last two decades of his life, Buckminster Fuller gave many lectures to enthusiastic audiences. Here he holds up a model of sticks that are held together by the wires that connect them.

live." Every human being should have that right. In truth, "wealth is as much everybody's as is the air and sunlight." Moreover, all this can be done without atomic power or fossil fuels. Energy will come from such sources as the sun, the waves, the tides, and the winds. If people cooperate as "one harmonious world family," all this can be done in ten years.

That was Fuller's vision. He was absolutely certain he was right. He had the facts to prove it. And he could show that such a Spaceship Earth could continue on and on. Treated with the respect a good home deserves, the earth will provide more and more. There will not, however, be more and more people. "The population explosion is a myth." As societies reach a high standard of living, the birthrate actually starts to decline. According to Fuller, humanity's numbers will level off at about 5 billion.

But wouldn't there be problems? How about all the idle people? Aren't idle people dangerous people? No, Fuller would say. There is no proof of that. In the past, idle people have often been fearful people. When fears about "earning a living" are gone, people will be free to use their minds and enjoy themselves. Learning and travel will become the ways of the future. For instance, the ancient cities of Greece and Rome could be rebuilt exactly as they were. Then people could travel in time as well as space. If someone wanted to, he or she could experience life in a medieval castle for a month or two. Today we worry about something called unemployment. Nonsense! Seen in the right way, unemployment is a plus, not a minus. It is humanity's hard-won right to be free from burdensome toil.

By 1980, both Bucky and Anne were slowing down. Actually, Anne's health started to go first. Allegra, of course, was concerned. As a professor of dance at the University of California, it wasn't easy for her to get away. Why didn't Bucky and Anne move to California, to be nearer Allegra and Bob? This is just what happened. The Fullers moved to Pacific Palisades, a Los Angeles suburb. Their house was just two blocks from the Snyders'. Jaime Snyder moved in with the eighty-five-year-old couple, to be of what help he could.

Fuller's office and staff, however, remained in Philadelphia. Moving it would be a problem. By that time, Fuller's Chronofile numbered 737 volumes. Each contained more than 300 pages. There were about 260,000 letters and 40,000 articles. There were hundreds of tapes and thousands of unpublished pages. Bucky decided to leave the treasure where it was. In his travels, he could easily visit Philadelphia when he wanted to.

Fuller went on traveling and speaking, on and on and on. Late in June 1983, a reporter from *The New Yorker* gave a good picture of a typical Fuller performance. Bucky appeared on the Hunter College stage with his grandson Jaime. It was midmorning when he started. "To Bucky's credit, virtually no one in a crowd of more than a thousand got up to leave as he wound his way through a list of topics that included (in chronological order) the East India Company, Thomas Malthus, royal blood, the discovery of X rays, electricity as invisible reality, mile-long radio waves, new alloys of metal, gills of fish, wings of birds, Johannes Kepler, the temporal versus the eternal, the large percentage of the human body that is water, the enormous stresses on ships at sea, why human beings are in the universe, stages in the patent process, eclipses of the moons of Jupiter, the bright star at the end of the Big Dipper handle, caterpillar metamorphosis, the Big Bang, DC-4 airplanes, the navigational abilities of South Sea islanders, a sphere painted on a pharaoh's forehead, the direction in which a tree falls, and Alexander the Great. And that was *before* lunch."

That was before lunch, and that was quite a show for a man of eighty-seven—particularly for a man with other things on his mind. Anne had already had two operations for cancer. For more than six months, she had been in and out of a Los Angeles hospital. Bucky tried to be at her side whenever he could.

On the morning of July 1, 1983, Bucky and Jaime visited Anne at the Good Samaritan Hospital. "Visited" isn't quite the right word. Anne had already lapsed into a coma. She was unconscious. After going out for lunch, Bucky returned to the intensive care unit alone. Sitting at Anne's side, he was hit by a sudden massive heart attack. In a very short time he was dead.

And just thirty-six hours later, Anne Hewlett Fuller joined her husband in death. Bucky might have liked it that way. He might have said, once again, "There's something of the miraculous in all that."

Important Dates

1895 R. Buckminster Fuller, Jr., is born in Milton, Massachusetts, the son of Richard and Caroline Fuller.

1899 Young Fuller's first pair of glasses corrects his extremely poor vision.

1904 Grandmother Andrews buys Bear Island off the coast of Maine.

1910 Fuller's father, after a long illness, dies on Bucky's fifteenth birthday.

1913 Fuller graduates from Milton Academy and enters Harvard in the fall.

1914 Expelled from Havard for "irresponsible behavior," Fuller works in a Canadian cotton mill for several months. He is readmitted to Harvard in the fall.

1915 Expelled again from Harvard, Fuller works as meat handler for Armour and Company in New York City.

1917 Fuller enlists in the navy for World War I service. He marries Anne Hewlett.

1918 Anne Hewlett Fuller gives birth to a daughter, Alexandra.

1919 Fuller resigns his commission as a lieutenant in the U.S. Navy because of Alexandra's poor health. He becomes assistant export manager for Armour.

1922 Alexandra's death devastates Fuller. He forms the Stockade Building System to manufacture and sell a new kind of building block.

1927 Forced out of Stockade, Fuller goes through an emotional crisis and nearly commits suicide. He dedicates his life to the service of humanity. A second daughter, Allegra, is born.

1929 The word "Dymaxion" becomes Fuller's trademark, and is first used for his revolutionary "House on a Pole."

1933 The Dymaxion Vehicle is designed and built.

1938 *Nine Chains to the Moon,* Fuller's first book, is published. He leaves a two-year stint at the Phelps Dodge Corporation to join the staff of *Fortune* magazine.

1941 Fuller gives up drinking and smoking.

1943 While working at the Bureau of Economic Warfare, Fuller develops the Dymaxion Map.

1944 Fuller moves to Wichita, Kansas, to produce a new version of the Dymaxion House. He abandons the project in 1946.

1949 The geodesic dome is successfully demonstrated at Black Mountain College.

1953 Fuller's first commercial dome is erected for the Ford Motor Company.

1959 Fuller becomes Research Professor at Southern Illinois University.

1962 Fuller is named Charles Eliot Norton Professor of Poetry at Harvard University.

1967 A huge Fuller dome is the hit of Expo '67 in Montreal.

1973 The Fullers move to Philadelphia, where Bucky is World Fellow in Residence at the University City Science Center.

1975 Fuller publishes *Synergetics,* a major work, with E. J. Applewhite.

1980 The Fullers move to Pacific Palisades, California.

1983 R. Buckminster Fuller and his wife, Anne Hewlett Fuller, die within thirty-six hours of each other.

Bibliography

Applewhite, E.J. *Cosmic Fishing: An Account of Writing* Synergetics *with Buckminster Fuller*. New York: Macmillan, 1977.

Fuller, R. Buckminster. *And It Came to Pass—Not to Stay*. New York: Macmillan, 1976.

Fuller, R. Buckminster, with Kiyoshi Kuromiya. *Critical Path*. New York: St. Martin's Press, 1981.

Fuller, [R.] Buckminster. *Grunch of Giants*. New York: St. Martin's Press, 1983.

Fuller, R. Buckminster, and Anwar Dil. *Humans in Universe*. New York: Mouton, 1983.

Fuller, R. Buckminster. *Ideas and Integrities*. Englewood Cliffs, N.J.: Prentice-Hall, 1963. Also in paperback.

Fuller, R. Buckminster. *Nine Chains to the Moon*. New York: J. B. Lippincott, 1938. Also in paperback.

Fuller, R. Buckminster. *Operating Manual for Spaceship Earth*. Carbondale, Ill.: Southern Illinois University Press, 1969. Also in paperback.

Fuller, R. Buckminster. *R. Buckminster Fuller on Education*. Amherst, Mass.: University of Massachusetts Press, 1979.

Fuller, R. Buckminster, with E. J. Applewhite. *Synergetics: Explorations in the Geometry of Thinking.* New York: Macmillan, 1975.

Fuller, R. Buckminster, with E.J. Applewhite. *Synergetics 2.* New York: Macmillan, 1979.

Fuller, R. Buckminster. *Utopia or Oblivion: The Prospects for Humanity.* Woodstock, N. Y.: Overlook Press, 1969. Also in paperback.

Hatch, Alden. *Buckminster Fuller: At Home in the Universe.* New York: Crown Publishers, 1974.

Kenner, Hugh. *Bucky: A Guided Tour of Buckminster Fuller.* New York: William Morrow, 1973. Also in paperback.

* Lord, Athena V. *Pilot for Spaceship Earth: R. Buckminster Fuller, Architect, Inventor, and Poet.* New York: Macmillan, 1978.

* Rosen, Sidney. *Wizard of the Dome: R. Buckminster Fuller, Designer for the Future.* Boston: Little, Brown, 1969.

Sieden, Lloyd Steven. *Buckminster Fuller's Universe: An Appreciation.* New York: Plenum Press, 1989.

* Snyder, Robert, ed. *R. Buckminster Fuller: An Autobiographical Monologue/Scenario.* New York: St. Martin's Press, 1980.

Additional information and educational materials can be secured from two organizations dedicated to the unfinished work of R. Buckminster Fuller:

Buckminster Fuller Institute
1743 South La Cienega Boulevard, Los Angeles, CA 90035
Phone: (213) 837-7710
Fax: (213) 837-7715

World Game Institute
University City Science Center
3508 Market Street, Philadelphia, PA 19104

* Readers of the Pioneers in Change book *Buckminster Fuller* will find this book particularly readable.

About the Author

R obert R. Potter served for three years in the United States Army during the Korean conflict, then got three degrees from Columbia University. His teaching career ranges from junior-high to graduate school. *Buckminster Fuller* is his sixteenth book. A native of Manhattan, Dr. Potter has spent the past twenty years with his family in West Cornwall, Connecticut. Membership in the Institute of General Semantics led him to a long-standing interest in the ideas of Buckminster Fuller.